MW00620322

*A voice from the East—a voice
from the West—a voice from the
far winds—a voice against the temple!
Woe! Woe! Woe! Jerusalem.*

The cover etching is a modification by Nevada artist Roy Purcell of a frieze depicting the Jewish captives as they entered Rome after their capture in AD 70 by the Roman general Titus at Jerusalem. In the procession are spoils taken from the Jewish temple – veils from the sanctuary, the seven-branched candlestick, a golden table, and books of the law. The original art is sculpted on the underside of the Arch of Titus in the Roman Forum. It is a silent witness of the fulfillment of Jesus' prophecy of the complete destruction of Jerusalem within a generation (Matthew 24, especially verse 34).

Published by Nevada Publications
Box 15444, Las Vegas, Nevada 89114
(702) 747-0800

Copyright © 1996 by Stanley W. Paher
ISBN 0-913814-40-7

Manufactured in the United States of America

MATTHEW 24

First Century Fufillment or End-Time Expectation?

STANLEY W. PAHER

LAS VEGAS
NEVADA PUBLICATIONS
1996

THE PLACE OF WAILING AT JERUSALEM – 1864 WOODCUT

TABLE OF CONTENTS

AUTHOR'S PREFACE

W<small>ARS AND RUMORS</small> of wars! Famines and earthquakes in diverse places . . . tribulations and apostasy, the gospel to all the world within a generation . . . false teachers to appear before the end . . . and, finally, the portentous abomination of desolation!

These utterances by Jesus just before his death – and recorded in Matthew 24 – have been sensationalized by modern media evangelists who apply all of them to the present time, as prelude to the end of the world and the second coming. Various millennialists promise that these "signs of the times" will tell when the "latter days" will be, so that the time of the return of Christ "on the clouds of heaven" can be calculated. At that time, there would be the gathering of the elect, the rapture of the saints in the sky, the Great Tribulation, and Christ's personal reign upon a renovated earth restored to the paradise of Eden.

In the millennialists' plan, the Jews must return to Jerusalem, rebuild the ancient temple, and restore Levitical animal sacrifices and ceremony. A revived Roman Empire consisting of ten kings (Rev. 17:3) would be established, in turn triggering a Russian invasion of the holy land (Ezek. 38:3f), to be stayed by the Lord Himself (v. 8). This scenario fails to consider the complete fulfillment of every figure from Matthew 24 in the turbulent years prior to the destruction of Jerusalem in AD 70.

Speculation about end-time events is nothing new. Just prior to the year 1000, many sold possessions and forgave debts before wandering to the mountaintops to await the Lord. The ruling Pope held a midnight mass on December 31 to usher in the end of the world. In the fifteenth century, John Wycliffe noted many earthquakes and epidemics, and thought that the world's end was near. Even Martin Luther, a century later, wrote that the judgment would soon come. Joseph Smith, William Miller, and Charles T. Russell, all set failed dates for the end.

Now, at the approach of a millennium in the year 2000, popular-religious writers are courting premillennial fundamentalists, who are eager to know the identity of the man of sin, the antichrist, and of the ancient biblical nations and their possible correspondence with modern ones. They have set new dates to mark the time of the generation of Matthew 24, so that the spiritual might be ready to rapture with the Lord and reign with him for the next 1,000 years.

Interpreters such as Hal Lindsey peruse the Bible to identify the end times, carefully analyzing horns, hoofs, and tails of biblical apocalyptic animal figures, seeking specific applications to near-future events. Every spring-time, they count buds on trees in anticipation of the "nearness" (Matt. 24:33) of all things mentioned by Jesus in Matthew 24. Millennial books contemplate the earth's final days, the countdown to the end, and tell of the world's appointment with destiny; they pointedly warn of the approaching storm, and ask if mankind will survive. Such "gloom and doom" creates despair but does not engender faith in God or encourage thoughtful study of the biblical doctrine of last things in literary and historical contexts.

Using the Old Testament and non-canonical works as precedent, this book shows that all ideas and symbols of Matthew 24 refer directly to ancient societies – especially to the Jewish nation which fell to the Romans in AD 70 – and demonstrate this in larger historical and literary contexts. All efforts to extend these prophecies to the present encounter immense difficulties.

～

Many individuals assisted in the preparation of this book. Upon its first edition, entitled *If Thou Hadst Known,* Yater Tant, Robert H. West, Don Bassett, Gary Henry, and Gordon Kirby made helpful comments. To this new expanded version renditions of scriptural passages were offered by the able minds of Guthrie Dean, Gene Peacock, Wanda Shirk, and Ron McRay; their thoughtful suggestions have added greatly to the value of the final result. Timely comment also came from Gary Cage and Michael Hall; Edward Fudge assisted in defining millennial beliefs.

Kathleen Manning of Antiquarian Books and Prints was helpful with illustrations, as was Homer Hailey, whose reading of the text improved the quality of its commentary on Matthew 24. Artist Roy Purcell's work graces the cover, to which K. C. Den Dooven offered technical assistance. Transcription of the original text into pages was done by Paul Cirac; the final cover composition and display typography is by Paul David Morrison. To one and all, my sincere thanks.

—Stanley W. Paher

STRUGGLE FOR THE PALM LEAVES – HARPER'S WEEKLY, 1878

Chapter One

INTRODUCTION

A T THE ANNUNCIATION of Jesus, the angel Gabriel told Mary that the child which she would bear "shall be called the Son of the Most High, and the Lord God shall give him the throne of his father David: and he shall reign over the house of Jacob forever, and of His kingdom there shall be no end" (Luke 1:32-33). The "kingdom" mentioned by Luke means the same as "reign," just as in the passage the words "forever" and "no end" are identical in concept. These sets of terms are synonymous through parallelism.

About the time of His ascension into heaven as witnessed by many disciples (Acts 1:9-11), where He took His seat at the right hand of God, Jesus began to exercise this authority as King of kings (Matt. 28:18-20). Christ Jesus continues to reign over His kingdom, His covenant people who have been called out of the realm of darkness into the world of marvelous light, where there is fellowship with God.

Luke's statement and the fulfillment in the resurrected Christ are the culmination of several marvelous prophetic truths which holy men had uttered for centuries. By the time of the Pentecost of Acts 2, the day of "beginning" (Acts 11:15) when the Holy Spirit was manifested, Peter and the other apostles began to preach the fundamental fact that Jesus had been raised from the dead to sit on David's throne (Acts 2:30, 36), because God had exalted Him in glory (John 7:39), majesty, and splendor to reside on His right hand as Prince and Savior.

For nearly two thousand years since that time of coronation (not inauguration, as if the kingdom were absolutely new among men), Jesus has been King above all others and Lord of lords, both in heaven and on earth, displaying His authority over angels and every other creature. He is the Judge of all, the living and the dead, the visible and invisible. All beings are subject to His reign – everything! He was given authority to rule until all enemies would be placed under His feet, the last of which would be death (I Cor. 15:24-26).

In opposition to this teaching, many modern evangelicals in varied forms propose the notion of an extravagant earthly kingdom with a reign of the saints and their yet future thousand-year reign with Jesus ruling over all the various cities and kingdoms of the world. Jesus Himself would sit upon a throne in the city of David, Jerusalem, heading a political government, just as monarchs function today. All such theories depend on ignoring Jesus' plain statement about the source and origin of God's reign: "My kingdom is not of this world" (John 18:36). Indeed, several of the Jewish prophets point to Christ's rule as being initiated in the first century, not in the future.

Some modern dispensational millennialists see this kingdom as postponed, because Christ's disciples allegedly rejected the spiritual kingdom, and so God had to substitute the "New Testament Church." Other millennialists see the delay as part of God's original plan to initiate the millennium at the end of history. In either case, most premillennial views attempt to initiate an earthly kingdom at a time much later than the book of

Acts reports that Christ ascended into heaven, so that He could begin His reign from heaven.

Advocates of a yet future earthly kingdom make special use of numerous biblical passages about the nature and place of Jesus' reign and the quality of His government. Several hundred years before the event, Isaiah foretold when the reign of Jesus would begin.

"For unto us a child is born, unto us a son is given; and the government shall be on his shoulders; and his name shall be called Wonderful, Counsellor, Mighty God, Everlasting Father, Prince of Peace. Of the increase of his government and of peace there shall be no end, upon the throne of David, and upon his kingdom, to establish it and to uphold it with justice and with righteousness from that time forth even forever" (9:6-7).

Daniel also prophesied of distinct qualities of the kingdom: "I saw in the night-visions, and, behold, there came with the clouds of heaven one like unto a Son of man, and he came even to the ancient of days, and they brought him near before him. And there was given him dominion, and glory, and a kingdom, that all the peoples, nations and languages should serve him: his dominion is an everlasting dominion, which shall not pass away, and his kingdom that which shall not be destroyed" (7:13-14).

In these two passages, Isaiah and Daniel identify the person and place of the reign, establish the fact of the reception by Christ of dominion, of glory and of the everlasting kingdom, and of the scope and breadth of His rule as including all nations and peoples, as well as the eternal character of the government — that it would be indestructible and not be subject to demise.

That the mid-first century saints were *in* the kingdom is reaffirmed by the author of Hebrews: "Wherefore, receiving a kingdom that cannot be shaken, let us have grace, whereby we may offer service to God with reverence and awe [godly fear] . . ." (12:26-28). God's people in Colossae understood that they had been translated into the kingdom of the son of God's love (1:13).

The subjects in the kingdom today coincide with the people of Christ, the *ekklesia,* the "New Testament Church." This kingdom is always near; there is not a time when its beginnings (or extension) are not manifest. There are absolutely no signs preceding it; Jesus called men away from idle speculation about anything signaling the arrival of the kingdom (Matt. 12:38-40, 16:1-4), for it "cometh not with observation," as if it were limited to a one-time occurrence. Rather, we should always behave like covenant people serving Christ and enjoying life in the kingdom (Matt. 25:1-30, Luke 12:35-46).

A proper conception of the kingdom, God's reign, is necessary to understand the difficult figure-laden passages of the apostolic writings, especially those involving prophecy. The Bible is often misunderstood because of the nature of its symbolic language. Another common flaw in interpretation is the failure to employ the Jewish writings as precedent to help interpret difficult New Testament passages. In insisting upon an earthly 1000 year reign, with Jesus governing from Jerusalem, millennialism in all forms fails in both of these points, in that their doctrinal systems are laden with misconceptions about Jesus' reign and the nature of the everlasting kingdom. To support their teachings, flamboyant dispensationalists give special meaning to controversial portions of the Bible such as Matthew 24, Mark 13, Luke 13, 17, and 21, and many other places throughout the gospel accounts.

Millennialists insist that Matthew 24 is the focal point of all Bible prophecy and that it tells of the coming of Jesus and the setting up of a yet-future earthly kingdom. These theorists look for worldwide catastrophe involving the heavenly bodies in convulsion, angels, lightning, clouds, trumpets, the winds, etc. (vv. 29-33). Preceding these events, everyone is to watch for the "signs of the times" – false teachers, wars, famines, earthquakes, a worldwide penetration of the gospel – after which would follow the famous great tribulation.

Such an interpretation brings almost insuperable difficulties. First of all, it ignores the coupling together of the two sections of Jesus' discourse, the signs of impending destruction described from verses 5 through 28 and the heavenly signs thereafter. Matthew 24:29 says that they will follow each other "immediately" – very soon afterwards.

The time frame of all these events is given in verse 34: "This generation shall not pass until *all* these things be fulfilled." Thus, every event of Matthew 24:5-33 would transpire during the approximate thirty seven years leading up to the fall of Jerusalem in AD 70. Most millennial dispensational teaching also leaves unexplained numerous other statements found throughout the gospels and apostolic teachings which sees a judicial coming of the Christ to close out the era of institutional Judaism in AD 70. Several dozen of these passages are commented upon throughout this book.

Clearly, Jesus was addressing an "adulterous and sinful generation," one which would live to see the end of their nation (Matt. 24:34, Mark 9:1). This generation of Jews was unfaithful because in the covenant they had committed every kind of sin specified by the Old Testament prophets. They had forsaken Yahweh as guide and forgotten their agreement with God.

The inevitable result had to be utter devastation, just as God had brought down Jerusalem because of unfaithfulness and apostasy more than 600 years previously. In fact, the end occurred within, though on the extreme edge of, the generation existing at the time of Christ. It was His presence *(parousia)* that gospel writers described as the coming of the Son of man, though sometimes writers used another Greek word, coming *(erchomai)*.

The apostles and other New Testament authors were steeped in the traditions of Palestinian Judaism, writing in the very shadow of the destruction of their city. Many of their readers had witnessed the long drawn-out agony of the five-year Jewish Wars during the years 66-70. The fortunes of

Jerusalem greatly color the synoptic gospels – Matthew, Mark, and Luke.

Such passages as Matthew 24 are properly understood only in their historical background – the setting behind the text. Many first century saints were familiar with the style and contents of some Old Testament material, as well as the apocryphal works written during the four hundred years before Jesus was born. All of these scriptures commonly shared the wealth of idioms, rhetorical expressions, similes, metaphors, and other types of symbolism, which Jewish prophets and scribes used liberally.

The figures of speech of Matthew 24 therefore find numerous counterparts throughout Jewish history. Various prophets ordinarily described divine intervention into national affairs as God coming in the clouds of heaven with his angels, announced by disturbances of heavenly bodies. Daniel tells of the Son of man "coming" to set up a universal kingdom, and the removal of perhaps its chief obstacle to fulfillment, party-oriented Judaism. The kingdom of Christ would survive the AD 70 event, replacing forever as obsolete any earthly notion that Israel was still God's people.

The initial announcement in common preaching that the kingdom was nigh, was about AD 30-31 in the Judean wilderness, when John the Baptist boldly went forth preaching, "Repent ye, for the kingdom of heaven [God's reign] is at hand" (Matt. 3:2). Jesus also proclaimed the same thing (Matt. 4:17). Joseph of Arimathea and others were "waiting for the kingdom of God" (Luke 23:51). This concept coincides with Simeon's "looking for the consolation of Israel" (Luke 2:25) or the "redemption of Jerusalem" (v. 38), the comfort which a relationship with Jesus would bring to each person personally.

During His ministry, Jesus continually warned the long-blessed nation of physical destruction that would befall it for refusing to enter the reign of the Son of David. As the ideal king, Jesus fulfilled the established Jewish conception of the Judge to come as "ruler of the kings of the earth" (Rev. 1:5,

12:5, 17:14), breaking the nations with a rod of iron (Psa. 110:5-6, 2:8-9).

Each gospel writer stressed this conception of Jesus Christ as Judge. The Son of man would come on the clouds of heaven (Matt. 26:64) to execute judgment in AD 70 upon disobedient, rebellious Jews (Matt. 16:27-28). This coming or presence (*parousia/erchomai*) would be preceded by definite signs, as mentioned in Matthew 24, all of which would be within the generation of Jesus' immediate disciples (v. 34). For more than a third of a century after Pentecost (Acts 2:1f), that kingdom would be tested in various localities by Gentile paganism and Christ-hating Jews; and because of the spiritual presence (coming) of Christ, it would emerge unshackled by Judaistic parties, after the debacle of AD 70.

Unfortunately, flesh-oriented Judaism saw nothing in the person of Jesus which corresponded to the pompous political notions which they had formed of the Christ. In contrast, faithful covenant Jews with pure hearts continued to strengthen their relationship with the God of heaven. Failing to perceive Jesus as this Holy One, the nation of Judea would ultimately cease to exist. The utter destruction of Jerusalem and its glorious temple in AD 70 proclaimed to the world that no other Christ should be anticipated, only the One who had come in judgment against these godless people, and who will come again to judge all sinners and save those who are His.

The fall of Jerusalem as well as the rest of Judea was the birth pangs of another renewed order, a watershed in God's relations with man. Orthodox Judaism (a term which means "the religion of the Jews"), the great hindrance to the full expansion of the kingdom of God, was severely crippled. Without the temple and a legitimate priesthood, the Jews quickly intensified their emnity for orthodox Christians, who in turn saw teachings of carnal Judaism to be strictly avoided. Thus began a cleavage which has never been repaired. After AD 70, God's covenant ones in Christ continued to suffer (just as disciples of

Christ had beforehand) unorganized and sporadic local persecution from Jewish partisans for still another half century, essentially until the time of the Bar-Kochba rebellion in Jerusalem in AD 133.

This coming, or the presence of the Son of man in AD 70, is therefore one significant occurrence of the coming of the kingdom. It is a "day of the Lord," a time of judgment which was preceded by tribulation and apostasy. During the years 66-70, Jerusalem was hopelessly trapped between starvation and military destruction. At the end of this time of unrest and ferment (that is, immediately, Matt. 24:29), the Jewish religious powers would shake. The tribes of the land would mourn, and the sign of the Son of man would appear in the political heaven (Judea), as He would come against faithless individuals on the clouds of judgment with power and great glory (Matt. 24:30-33). In the year 70, Jesus demonstrated His kingly glory as he wielded divine authority and power, coming against religiously and socially corrupt Jerusalem, using the Roman armies as the instrument of His wrath.

And so, to misunderstand the meaning of these common Hebrew figures such as the clouds, the heavens, the day of the Lord, the coming, trumpets, winds, the sea, rock, vine, etc., is to fail to grasp the intention of the gospel writers in respect to the kingdom: its spiritual nature and the fact that Jesus is *presently* King of kings ruling over the hearts of His subjects, the body of Jesus Christ. He now serves in the same capacity as had God when He presided over the kingdom throughout the Old Testament period of history.

A misuse of these symbols has led to mistaken conclusions about the nature of Christ's reign. Without regard to scripture precedent, many contemporary millennialists assign various prophecies to the future "second coming" of Christ. The rest of this study will review several dozen prophetic passages which have already been fulfilled in the latter days of the Jewish kingdom, in those years of the Jewish Wars in AD 66-70, culminating in the destruction of Jerusalem.

Chapter Two

THY KING COMETH

O N THE MORNING of Jesus' triumphal entry into Jerusalem, traditionally thought to be the Sunday before His crucifixion, He was accompanied by a throng of emotionally charged followers. With their hopes fired by the wonderful miracles wrought by the prophet from Galilee, they had gathered on the Bethany road to escort Jesus into Jerusalem. With less than a mile to go He stopped in sight of the city. The gilded roofs of its temple and the gleam of its marble walls spread out before Him, beyond the brown-green expanse of the valley of the Kidron.

The Master's eyes, fired by the truths in the Jewish prophetic writings, saw beyond the shimmering sight before Him to the terrible destruction which, within a generation, would level the city. As He gazed upon Jerusalem, Jesus wept over it. He said plaintively, "If thou hadst known in this day, even thou, the things which belong unto peace! But now they are hid from thine eyes. For the days shall come upon thee, when thine enemies shall cast ramparts about thee, and encircle thee and keep thee on every side, and shall hurl thee to the ground, and thy children within thee; and they shall not leave in thee one stone upon another, because thou knewest not the time of thy visitation"(Luke 19:41-44).

These somber words of portent and power were literally fulfilled about 37 years later, in AD 70, when General Titus' Roman legions utterly destroyed the glorious city. This event climaxed five years of hopeless revolts involving two attempts by the Roman leaders to take Jerusalem, and continual suicidal strife among warring Jewish factions. Many acclaim the Jewish Wars as among the greatest of all recorded struggles of mankind. Certainly none other can match the horror of it, and the misery and suffering brought about by wholesale and indiscriminate slaughter of both soldiers and civilians.

The Jews initially revolted soon after Herod's death (Acts 12:23), in about AD 44; full-scale war finally broke out in the year 66, with unexplainable success by the Jews against the Roman military led by Cestius Gallus. Vespasian came upon Jerusalem two years later, overrunning the countryside ahead of him, devastating the land until it was utterly desolate. Incredibly, terror reigned in the city and faction fighting used up the limited amounts of food, clothing and other resources.

Though Vespasian withdrew to become emperor early in AD 70, his son Titus led the Roman battalions into Judea in the spring of 70 to subdue the Jews. In the interim, the three major parties in Jerusalem intensified their infighting. Even as the Romans descended upon the city with all fury, the Jewish political factions continued internal warfare.

In a momentary respite from Roman pressure in April, about 200,000 Jews from throughout the world entered the city to worship at the time of unleavened bread. Soon, however, the Roman legions sealed off Jerusalem, shutting up as in a prison many of the new arrivals with the 50,000 resident population. The sentries allowed no provisions to pass them to reinforce the hapless population, which could not escape from the city, because one Jewish leader sealed the gates, and killed all who attempted to flee.

The Romans next began to erect huge platforms to bear upon the walls. By the month of May they mastered the two north walls and took the northern part of the city. At one time during the long summer, Titus briefly suspended military action to afford the Jews a chance to surrender, since famine began to creep up on them. But they refused. Titus then pressed his attack, next conquering the fortress of Antonia and the lower city. Its buildings were leveled or set ablaze.

Late in August the Roman battering crews finally cracked the most difficult obstacle in Jerusalem, the series of citadel walls. The magnificent temple was looted and razed to the ground, virtually stone by stone. On the morning of September 8, the sun rose over Jerusalem in flames. About two weeks later the upper city was mastered, and Jerusalem was fully under Roman control. The Romans set up their standards on the towers of the upper city and sacrificed to pagan gods. While some of the soldiers clapped and sang victory chants, others sacked and burned buildings throughout the city.

The contemporary Jewish historian Josephus concluded: "No destruction ever wrought by God or man approached the wholesale carnage of this war. . . Everyone was either taken prisoner or instantly killed in their tracks." He wildly estimated that 97,000 were led away in chains as captives and that 1,100,000 perished in the long siege.

Previous to the Jewish War, many who had seen Jerusalem envied the city because the true God had endowed it with so many blessings. But, wrote Josephus, the city "deserved these terrible misfortunes on no other account than that she produced a generation such as brought about her ruin." Earlier, in comparing Jerusalem with Sodom, the historian said that Jerusalem "produced a generation far more godless than those who perished thus [by hail in Sodom], a generation whose mad folly involved the nation to ruin." Josephus' conclusion may be questionable, since epidemic homosexuality caused Sodom's destruction, and not even ten righteous people could be found there. Were there ten people of faith in Jerusalem at its destruction? (Luke 18:8).

Therefore the destruction of Jerusalem, regarded by many historians as one of the world's most notable events, is a strong, consistent biblical theme, from Moses to the author of the book of Hebrews. Indeed, an often overlooked aspect of Jesus' earthly mission was to deliver His faithful from the oppression of the prevailing institutional hierarchy, and, as a display of divine vengeance, punish an evil generation of Talmudic Jews, which had become a fallen, disobedient people by the time of Christ. All was to take place according to various biblical statements that declare His influence in the event.

Numerous prophetic passages, especially those in Deuteronomy, Isaiah, Daniel, Malachi and Joel, and also utterances by Jesus in the gospels, foretell every aspect of the destruction of Jerusalem: the setting in a time of unrest, the great tribulation, the siege of the city, the escape of faithful messianic Jews, the toppling of buildings, the immense suffering, the violent killing of thousands of Jews, the enslavement of many others, and the end of the nation.

Religious speculators overlook these positive, direct fulfillments of the prophets, in favor of end time applications prior to a yet-future "second coming" of Christ, when He allegedly will set up a thousand year reign over His saints on the earth, a materialistic political and not a spiritual rule. This premillennial theory almost invariably describes Christ as "coming amid tribulations," and various signs would foretell the end of the age. Yet, several scriptures show different "comings" of Christ.

In Luke 19:41-44, Jesus said that He Himself would "visit" Jerusalem at the time when the great physical calamities mentioned would take place. Yet the Romans actually carried out the siege, loss of life, and destruction of the city and temple. In what way can these statements be reconciled? This "visitation" is evidently a manifestation of

Christ's rule, or divine spiritual presence, in the kingdoms of men. The coming of Christ is His *parousia*, or divine presence —literally "to be with." It is a spiritual influence, not a physical manifestation (see Chapter Six).

Old Testament Comings of the Lord

As "King of the nations" (Jer. 10:7), Yahweh presided over all ancient earthly kingdoms, and set up as rulers whomsoever He willed, a truth forcefully taught by Daniel (see 4:25, 32b; 5:18, 21b). Isaiah shows that God raised up Assyria to punish Israel (10:5-7), employed Babylon to subdue Judah (39:1-8), and later stirred up the Medo-Persians to destroy Babylon (13:17; see also 29:6).

Isaiah said that "Yahweh rideth upon a swift cloud and cometh unto Egypt" (19:1). On that occasion God visited the idolatrous Egyptians in judgment. In mercy, Yahweh would visit Ashkelon (Zeph. 2:4-7). Moses wrote that in the days of Egyptian bondage "the people believed: and when they heard that Yahweh had visited the children of Israel, and that He had seen their affliction, then they bowed their heads and worshipped" (Ex. 4:31; see also 3:18). The psalmist asked God to "look down from heaven, and behold, and visit this vine [His people]" (80:14). In none of these physically observable historical events did God actually appear on earth, though He of course was personally invisible in them.

These "comings" of deity are often associated with the clouds, as in Isaiah 19:1, quoted above. Ezekiel plainly connects clouds with divine power executed in judgment. "Wail ye, alas for the day!" said Yahweh. "For the day is near, even the day of Yahweh is near; it shall be a day of clouds, a time of the nations. And a sword shall come upon Egypt, and anguish shall be in Ethiopia, when the slain shall fall in Egypt; and they shall take away her multitude, and her foundations shall be broken down" (30:3-4).

Verse five mentions several Egyptian allies that would meet a similar fate, while verse eight foretells that Egyptian cities would be wasted: "And they shall know that I am Yahweh, when I have set a fire in Egypt, and all her helpers are destroyed." Verse ten names Nebuchadrezzar as the conqueror, but only with God's approval, according to chapter 29:19-20. There, God said that He would "give the land of Egypt unto Nebuchadrezzar, king of Babylon; and He shall carry off her multitude, and take her spoil, and take her prey; and it shall be the wages for his army. I have given him the land of Egypt as his recompense for which he served, because they wrought for me, saith the Lord Yahweh" (see also 30:19). The king himself later plainly acknowledged that his power came from above (Dan. 5:21b). Jesus also told Pilate the same thing (John 19:11).

Calamities of nature also signified God's judgments and His presence among men. At Mt. Sinai, thunders, lightnings, and a thick cloud appeared as a result of Yahweh's "coming" among the wicked Israelites (Ex. 19:16ff). The mountain quaked greatly because of God's majestic presence (vv. 18; see also Isa. 64:1-3). The writer of Hebrews said that all of these things served as a warning to sinful Israelites (12:18, 25-26). David said that thunder and hailstones were a response from Yahweh (Psa. 18:13).

On another occasion, Isaiah promised that God would visit the Israelite nation with thunder, earthquake, flames of fire, noise, and a whirlwind because of their wickedness (29:6). These words indicate judgment. The heavens trembled and the earth shook when God visited Babylon in judgment (Isa. 13:13). Haggai wrote that while judging the nations, God would shake the heavens, the earth, the sea and the dry land (2:6, 21).

Early saints in Christ and the Lord Himself naturally employed, both in speech and in writing these long-established idioms and figures to describe an outpouring of divine power in their day. Such a use of language is the essence of communication, selecting concepts that readers can understand. The

New Testament throughout makes frequent use of the words coming, presence, visitation (in Luke 19:44), clouds, and all sorts of natural calamities. Various millennial theorists nearly always associate these words with the final end time return of Christ, popularly referred to as the "second coming." But these phrases nearly always have special figurative meanings, and a failure to note them leads to confusion.

For instance, the New Testament tells of a number of "comings" of the Lord. Jesus' initial mission among man was a coming or appearance (II Tim. 1:10). Jesus spoke of the outpouring of the Holy Spirit as a divine coming (John 14:18, 28). He comes in loving manifestation to anyone who keeps his word (John 14:23), a spiritual presence. He came by the gospel, preaching peace to the Gentiles (Eph. 2:17).

To the Asian *ekklesiai* Ephesus, Pergamum and Sardis late in the first century, Jesus would come in chastisement (Rev. 2:5, 16; 3:3); He admonished readers in Thyatira and Philadelphia to "hold fast till I come" (Rev. 2:25, 3:11); to the Laodiceans He said He would come and sup with them (Rev. 3:20). The destruction of Jerusalem in AD 70 was a similar manifestation of the Lord coming in judgment.

The last of all "comings" will be the Lord's yet future final return (I Cor. 15:12-58, I Thess. 4:13-5:11). When New Testament writers spoke of it, more often than not they used the word "appearing" (such as in I Tim. 6:14; II Tim. 4:1, 8; Tit. 2:13; I Pet. 1:7, and elsewhere), or expressions that denote a visible presence (Acts 1:11), as used in connection with the first coming, His entrance into this world (John 1:14, II Tim 1:10).

Hebrews 9:26-28 is typical of these: ". . .but now once, at the end of the ages, hath he been manifested to put away sin by the sacrifice of Himself. And inasmuch as it is appointed unto men once to die, and after this cometh judgment; so Christ also, having been once offered to bear the sins of many, shall appear a second time, apart from sin, to them that wait for Him, unto salvation."

Man *dying* once and then entering judgment is juxtaposed with Christ being *offered* once on the cross and then appearing before God's judgment to present the perfect life of obedience which He offered on the cross. Just as Jesus lived and died as our representative high priest, so He will finally come in glory to consummate all blessings which He has secured for His covenant people. As One vindicated by His resurrection, Christ will return personally and visibly, a presence or coming quite distinct from the other "comings" mentioned above. Maranatha! Come, Lord Jesus!

Since the language employed in describing the final yet future appearance of Jesus is similar to the figures describing the destruction of Jerusalem, and the other biblical "comings," it is necessary to study carefully the passages relating to each. Failing to distinguish between these comings, many religious speculators confuse them.

Indiscriminately, they build a religious doctrine around a system of signs which would allegedly precede the final return of Jesus Christ. In sharp contrast to His first ministry, His "coming" in the gospel, His coming to the churches in Revelation, etc., Jesus plainly said that His future final coming would be completely unheralded, with *no* signs (Matt. 25:31-46).

Other than general exhortations to live in daily expectation of His return, the scriptures that refer to the final coming are those concerning the events that will take place at the end time. These are the resurrection of the dead, (I Cor. 15:21-23), the changing of the living (I Cor. 15:51-54, I Thess. 4:17f), the great day of the judgment (John 5:28-29, Acts 17:31, Rom. 2:16), and the final destruction of the world (Matt. 25:31-46).

Contrary to the premillennial theory of two resurrections over time—that the saints would rise first, and the sinners later, after the one millennium of a literal one thousand years—there is only one for both the just and unjust, described as *the* resurrection (John 11:24, Acts 24:15; see also Acts 23:6, Phil. 3:11).

"But as touching the resurrection of the dead, have you not read that which was spoken unto you by God, saying, 'I am the God of Abraham, and the God of Isaac, and the God of Jacob?' God is not the God of the dead, but of the living." was Jesus' response to the Sadducees, exposing their ignorance of the after-life (Matt. 22:31-32, see also Luke. 20:35).

As One possessing all authority (Matt. 28:18), Jesus the Christ presently rules the nations with a rod of iron (Psa. 2:8-9, 45:5-6, 110:5-6; Micah 5:15; Rev. 1:5, 12:5). Jesus is far above all other governance; everything is in subjection under His feet (Eph. 1:21-22; see also Rev. 5:13 and I Cor. 15:20-28). The Messiah will be eternally "King of kings and Lord of lords" (Rev. 19:15-16, 22:5). Further, since there are many "comings" of Yahweh in Old Testament times, is it not reasonable to conclude that there are many comings of Christ throughout New Testament times as well?

Just as surely as Jesus will return again in judgment to reward and punish, the apostles and gospel writers also taught that he participated in the destruction of Jerusalem through a "visitation," or a coming in divine judgment, using the Roman legions in AD 70. This spiritual presence was an execution of vengeance against a wicked generation of Jews that had rejected Him, as prophesied far in advance by holy men of God. Chapter Six fully develops the nature of this significant "coming," and Jesus' execution of divine vengeance, as King of kings.

JERUSALEM IN HER FALL – HARPER'S WEEKLY, 1872

Chapter Three

OLD TESTAMENT PROPHECIES
OF JERUSALEM'S DESTRUCTION

I N OLD TESTAMENT TIMES, God came upon wicked nations and visited them in judgment. Many of the
prophets used celestial objects and natural calamities to express
Yahweh's vexations and divine wrath. God did not exempt
His chosen Israel from destruction, if they pursued a course of
disobedience. Moses explicitly tells of the terrible end of a
degenerate nation.

Written at least 1,400 years before the time of Christ,
Deuteronomy 28 plainly tells about the fate of Israel over the
centuries. It would be set high above other nations and highly
blessed (vv. 1-14), if it "should hearken diligently unto the
voice of Yahweh thy God." In the rest of the chapter, Moses
fully described the fearful consequences of disobedience and
God's invoking of covenant curses after each of Israel's
apostasies, including the degeneration of Judea before AD 70.

If rebellion was pursued, curses would come upon the Jewish people (vv. 15-16), in the city and in the field (compare
with Ezek. 7:15 and Matt. 24:17-18). Disease would come

upon them (Deut. 28:22, 27-28), and also the sword, a foreign power, which proved to be various nations, including the Assyrians in 721 B.C., the Babylonians in 586 B.C., and ultimately the Roman Empire in the Christian era. Leviticus 26:25 says that the sword "shall execute the vengeance of the covenant." At that time there would be a scarcity of food.

Israel's sons and daughters thus would periodically be taken into captivity and slavery (Deut. 28:41,48). Its agressors would come from afar, "from the end of the earth, as the eagle flieth; a nation whose tongue thou shalt not understand (v. 49). In AD 70 the Roman armies swiftly descended upon hapless and spiritually desolate Jerusalem. It is merely a coincidence that the Romans had an eagle as a battle ensign.

Moses further described the future invaders as a nation with a "fierce countenance" (v. 50), denoting cruelty, as with the Assyrians, the Babylonians, and the Syrian, Antiochus Epiphanes. The Romans unrelentingly slaughtered the Jews in the capture of Jerusalem. Verses 52-57 graphically describe the siege – the walls would come down, in which they had trusted (for the institutional Jews had lost their trust in God), and the gates would be hemmed in. Family members would be at enmity against each other, and they would covet food. "And thou shalt eat the fruit of thine own body . . . " Since all of these things were fulfilled over and over in Israel's history and so literally in AD 70, Moses might well be mistaken for a perpetual eyewitness.

The eating of human flesh resulted when God imparted the severest degree of punishment for disobedience (Lev. 26:27-29). Cannibalism of babies occurred in Samaria, the capital of the Northern Kingdom, during the period of the Syrians (II Kgs. 6:28-29), and in Jerusalem when Nebuchadnezzar of Babylon took the city in 586 B.C. (Lam. 2:20, 4:10; Jer. 19:9). Apparently it was practiced just as appallingly during Titus' siege of Jerusalem in AD 70.

Finally, Moses said that the Jews would be tossed to and fro among all of the kingdoms of the earth (Deut. 28:25).

"Yahweh will scatter thee among all peoples from one end of the earth even unto the other end . . . And among these nations shall thou find no ease, and there shall be no rest for the sole of thy foot . . ." (Deut. 28:64-65; see also Lev. 26:31-33, Deut. 4:27). After the ten tribes of Israel fell in 721 B.C. and Judea was overrun 140 years later, God's people have been relocated by conquerors, just as Moses had predicted. The Jewish historian Josephus said that the Romans upon taking Jerusalem in AD 70 shipped thousands of Jews to Egypt and other Roman provinces to be sold into a life of bondage (see Deut. 28:68).

Over the centuries up to the final fulfillment of Moses' words in AD 70, the Jews have found no rest, as Jeremiah prophesied (4:27, 5:10-11, 30:11, 46:28). Both he and Moses taught that the land of Judah should become a desolation after each military conquest, but that there would be no *full end* to the Jews.

With what exactness have the prophecies in Deuteronomy come to pass! Written in the wilderness of Moab, before the children of Israel had secured the promised land of Palestine, Moses essentially foretold the fate of the chosen people, if they would ever become rebellious. Even today, Jews are persecuted in many countries, and the tiny modern state of Israel (which has *no* biblical connection with ancient Israel, nor any provable physical or genetic connection) must always be alert to keep from being overrun by its Arab neighbors.

The prophet anticipated that the people would corrupt themselves after his death (Deut. 31:29), adding "evil will befall you in the latter days." In Moses' song to the assembly of Israel (Chapters 32-33), he bluntly described the Jews living in the time of the degradation: "They are a perverse and crooked generation" (32:5, 20; compare with Acts 2:40, Matt. 17:17).

Since the Israelites had provoked God to anger with their vanities, He would bring the Gentiles into His family (Deut. 32:21b; Rom. 10:19-21). God promised bitter destruction, and the Jews would be scattered afar (v. 26) in their day of calamity (v. 35). The enemy would act swiftly against them in a time of vengeance (v. 35b), for God would no longer be their protector (v. 38). The events associated with the destruction of Jerusalem both in 586 B.C. and AD 70 adequately fulfill the portentous warnings contained in the Song of Moses.

Zachariah 14

Zechariah 14 may well refer to Rome's conquest of apostate Jerusalem in AD 70, for the imagery is appropriate. The day of Yahweh (v. 1), is an expression denoting a time of temporal judgment. In the composition of the Roman army (v. 2), all nations did battle Jerusalem. The city was taken, houses rifled, women ravished, and a considerable number were led into captivity. Similar events took place during the destruction of Babylon in about 540 B.C. (Isa. 13:9, 15-16). Earlier, in about 721 B.C., God had employed the Assyrians as a rod of His anger and indignation, to punish the ten northern tribes of Israel (Isa. 10:5).

The phrase "And His feet shall stand in that day upon the Mount of Olives . . ." (v. 4), if applicable to first century events, may refer to the Roman armies [God's feet] encamped in battle lines; interestingly, Jesus also stood on Mt. Olivet when he prophesied the doom of the city (Matt. 24:3f). The last part of verse 7 foretells the diffusion of knowledge after the AD 70 event; verses 8 and 9 note Christ's gospel and the cosmopolitan *ekklesia* and its success. All of these events are closely associated, because of the phrase "in that day" (vv. 4, 6, 8, 9; see also 1, 20). Further, the living waters of verse 8 correspond nicely with the waters of Ezekiel 47:1-12 and the apostle John's waters which flowed through the new Jerusalem (Rev. 22:1-2; see also John 7:38-39).

The catastrophic language of Zechariah 14 does not describe events surrounding a future "second coming" of Christ, as the premillennialists contend. In accordance with the common use of figurative language, Zechariah's imagery, such as the dividing of the Mount of Olives, the removal of mountains, and the opening of valleys, refers to common political events, and not to a future geographical renovation of Palestine in anticipation of a future thousand year reign of Christ.

Like Zachariah, Isaiah graphically described the simple, unpretentious mission of John the Baptist as a process of exalting every valley and leveling every mountain and hill (40:3-5; see also Luke 3:4-6). In exuberant language, the prophet told of the smoothing of the road for the Christ-King, Jesus: "Every valley shall be filled, and every mountain and hill shall be brought low; and the crooked shall become straight and the rough ways smooth."

The nation Israel was to assist in removing any spiritual barrier that might hinder His coming. Israel failed in this obligation; instead of flattening mountains and filling in ravines to make a proper messianic highway, the various Jewish religious party leaders set up roadblocks for the King. They did not remove moral obstacles, failing to repent at the preaching of John. The nation would suffer punishment within a generation, just as Zechariah had foretold, through the disruption of families by Roman military conquest of Judea in AD 70.

Isaiah

As a prophet of the Assyrian period, Isaiah also wrote about the terrible events prior to the ultimate fall of the nation. He declared that part of the Messiah's work was the proclamation of God's "day of vengeance" (61:2, 63:4). Those that mourn would be comforted and not forsaken (62:12), but the disobedient would perish (60:12). Judah's stay and staff (3:1) were taken away during the siege under Nebuchadnezzar in 586 B.C., and generally in the days of the Romans under Titus in the year 70.

The invasion described at 29:2-8 was not fully realized in the Assyrian Sennacherib's march upon Jerusalem in about 701 B.C., but in the Roman siege: "then will I distress Ariel [Jerusalem], and there shall be mourning and lamentation . . . and I will encamp against thee round about, and will lay siege against thee with posted troops, and I will raise siege works against thee. And thou shall be brought down." With language of judgment, Isaiah promised that, "She [Jerusalem] shall be visited of Yahweh of hosts with thunder, and with earthquake, and great noise, with whirlwind and tempest, and the flame of a devouring fire (v.6)."

Isaiah thus used common Jewish literary expressions to tell of the fall and destruction of the city. As shown previously, deity can visit earthly nations in a spiritual sense, as God did Egypt (Isa. 19:1). The thunder, earthquake, noise and flames express God's wrath, as in Isaiah 13:13, 64:3, Psalm 18:13, and elsewhere. Any application to a future "second coming" ignores historical fulfillments, and is not perceived as a direct warning to the generations in Jerusalem after Isaiah's day and before or during the time of Christ in the first century.

The New Heavens and New Earth

Isaiah 51:16, 65:17-66:24 tells of the manifold blessings which would come to the Jewish remnant in exile after their return from Babylon: "For behold, I create new heavens and a new earth; and the former things shall not be remembered, nor come into mind . . . For I will create Jerusalem to be a delight and its people a joy . . . For as the new heavens and the new earth, which I shall make, shall remain before me, saith Yahweh, so shall your seed and your name remain" (65:17-18, 66:22).

Isaiah is giving to Israel a glorious picture of their return from Babylonian exile, "in the new heavens and the new earth." Stripped of symbolism, this phrase means that one system would take the place of another, as it does in other biblical occurances (Matt. 24:36, II Pet. 3:13, Rev. 21:1, 4b). The passing of heavens and earth points to the end of the political order (Joel 3:14-17). Returning from Babylonian exile to their homeland, Israel would be abundantly blessed and would experience a new economy in which to keep God's ways, is Isaiah's declaration. But a restored people in Jerusalem after the exile and ultimately in the messianic era points to an even greater Jerusalem yet future (Rev. 21-22).

Even amid this optimism, the prophet warned of a falling away and judgment, which ultimately was realized in the destruction of Jerusalem in AD 70 – the cessation of an old order of things and the inauguration of another one. Isaiah presents the figure of a parent, with hands extended, as if appealing to wayward children (65:2). The plea is to the rebellious Jewish nation, which Paul called "disobedient and gainsaying" when he quoted the first two verses of Isaiah 65 in his letter to the Romans (10:20-21). The Pharisees and other Jewish parties would be cast off, because they stubbornly refused to heed the numerous appeals to repent by Jesus Christ and others sent from God, including John the Baptist. "O Jerusalem, Jerusalem, that killeth the prophets, and stoneth them that are sent unto her! How often would I have gathered thy children together, even as a hen gathereth her chickens under her wings, and ye would not," pleaded the Master, as He oft admonished the various Jewish leaders to turn to the living God from their handed-down religious practices (Matt. 23:37, Mark 7:9).

Yahweh renders recompense to His enemies, including the apostate Jews, amid the voices from the city and the temple (Isa. 66:6). Verses 15 and 16 assure that Yahweh will come with fire "to render His anger with fierceness, and His rebuke with flames of fire. For by fire will Yahweh execute judgment, and by His sword upon all flesh." In precisely this way Jerusalem was destroyed in AD 70.

Yet, for faithful covenant people after the captivity, and for righteous Jews and Gentiles and Jews in the messianic era, there would be abundant blessings, like a bubbling fountain where there is neither youth or age, and no weeping, for Yahweh would create "new heavens and a new earth" (Isa. 65:17-18; 66:22). There would be still another even greater spiritual renewal under the Messiah (John 4:24), displacing the older political order of the Israelite kingdom amid the heathen nations. Yahweh tells of the judgment upon the disobedient, for God's people as first century Zion would "go forth, and look upon the dead bodies of the men that have transgressed against me" (66:24; see also Psa. 110:6). These corpses include the disobedient and rebellious Christ-rejecting Jews of the generation of Jerusalem's destruction.

The scriptural references of Moses, Zechariah, David and Isaiah do not identify nations, events, or persons associated with the destruction of Jerusalem. Those prophets *generally* foretold the end of the Jewish state and the accompanying siege, tribulation, the scattering of Jews, and the fact that all these things would be manifestations of God's vengeance and wrath. Three other prophets, however, refer unmistakably to *specific* events that would precede the end of the Jewish state in the year 70: Joel, Malachi and Daniel.

Joel

"And it shall come to pass afterward (the last days – Acts 2:17), " said Joel, "that I will pour out my spirit upon *all* flesh; and your sons and your daughters shall prophesy, your old men shall dream dreams, your young men shall see visions: and also upon the servants and upon the handmaids in those days will I pour out my Spirit" (2:28-29). Thus, *all* of the people of Israel would potentially benefit, perhaps as Moses had wished, not merely a select group like the seventy in the earlier time (Num. 11:16f).

These words specifically apply to the miraculous events on Pentecost (Acts 2:1-4) in about AD 33 and in other events in the history of first century Jews. Though Joel's prophecy is often thought to embrace Gentiles (such as the outpouring of the Spirit upon the household of Cornelius in Acts 10:44), the *all flesh* of Joel seems to answer the limited spiritual experience in Moses' time, even as the *no flesh* of Matthew 24:22 applies only to the Jews in the great tribulation upon Jerusalem prior to AD 70.

Besides the outpouring of the Spirit and prophesying, the prophet also figuratively described associated events: "And I will show wonders in the heavens and in the earth: blood, and fire and pillars of smoke. The sun shall be turned into darkness, and the moon into blood, before the great and terrible day of Yahweh come . . . and it shall be, that whosoever shall call on the name of the Lord shall be delivered; for in Mount Zion and in Jerusalem there shall be those that escape" 2:30-32).

Millennialists admit to at least an indirect application of Joel's passage to the Pentecost of Acts 2, though looking for its final and even greater fulfillment in the "last days" in a yet-future "second coming." This view is contrary to Peter's teaching in Acts 2:17-21, where he quoted Joel's prophecy in reference to the outpouring of the spirit with its accompanying miracles on that Pentecost, and declared "this is that which was spoken by the prophet Joel." Since the *first* part of Joel's prophecy announces the beginning of the time of gospel preaching, and Peter declares the fulfillment, the *last* part of the same prophetic utterance must of necessity, by the principle of correspondence, be applied to the same period.

Joel's "day of the Lord," in consistent Hebrew prophetical usage, denotes a time period when Yahweh would render divine judicial destruction. It is a time of overthrowing of powers and ordinances, as in Isaiah 13, where identical figures describe ancient Babylon's destruction. Zephaniah's "great day of Yahweh" (1:14) also tells of the time when God's wrath would come upon Judah. It would be a day of terror and vengeance upon the disobedient when punishment would be rendered to them, though for the righteous it would be a day of deliverance from oppression. The tribulation prior to the fall of Jerusalem, AD 66–70, adequately fulfills such a time.

The day of the Lord is a day of decision for Yahweh (Joel 3:14), bringing darkness (Amos 5:18–20). The day of the Lord's vengeance of Isaiah 34:8 was similarly a local judgment against Edom and Bozrah (v. 7) couched in symbolic language, where streams would turn into pitch, and the land into an unquenchable blazing pitch. "The smoke thereof shall go up forever, from generation to generation it shall lie waste . . . " (v.10). Such radical, seemingly universal language does not describe literal world events but those in the two named heathen nations, properly pointing to God's intervention of judgment in a localized area.

Thus, if the Jews living prior to AD 70 would repent and turn toward righteousness, and again earnestly serve God, He would spare them from the tribulation attendant to the war upon Judea. But if they remained disobedient, they would be as an enemy, in the day of the Lord. The rebellious people would be conquered, but the faithful would be provided a way of escape and given safety (Joel 2:32). Indeed, in Matthew 24 Jesus provided numerous signs to His people, so that they could know when and how to flee from spiritually degenerate Jerusalem.

Therefore, Peter's use of Joel stood as a warning to first century Jews, who saw within a generation the end of their nation at the hands of Rome. Indeed, in AD 70, Judea's sun would set, as the Jewish order would be removed from among the earthly kingdoms.

Malachi

Among the last of the Jewish writing prophets, Malachi also used the phrase "great and terrible day" (4:5) and, as in Joel, it is a day of judgment upon the Jewish nation. The context begins at 3:17; there Yahweh promises to bring a day of judgment, one which "burneth as a furnace and all the proud and all that work wickedness shall be stubble. The day that cometh shall burn them up, sayeth Yahweh of hosts, that it shall leave them neither root nor branch" (4:1).

This powerful metaphor describes the day in which God will destroy proud works; it is a pronouncement of judgment against the generation of disorderly Jews, which had rejected the Christ and persecuted His followers. That the day shall leave neither root nor branch assures that the destruction will be complete – none shall escape. The wicked shall be as ashes after having been burnt with the fire of judgment (v. 3).

Out of this spiritual darkness Malachi looked confidently to the appearance of "Elijah," who would come before that day of judgment (4:5). Millennialists believe that the primary fulfillment will occur just before Christ's "second coming" when a literal, personal Elijah will appear on earth. To them the arrival of Jesus or John the Baptist, prior to the destruction of Jerusalem, merely served as an earnest of a yet future coming. Such a dual interpretation, featuring a fulfillment in a biblical event and still yet future in connection with a thousand-year earthly millennial reign, is in fact religious speculation. It is contrary to the recurring biblical pattern of a successive fulfillment of a Jewish prophet's words, first within the experience of his own or subsequent generation(s) and then again in the first century messianic era.

Contrary to this view, Jesus made it quite clear that this "Elijah" is himself by saying that "Elijah shall first come and restore all things" (Matt 17:11), a statement made after John the Baptist had died and is often applied to him. But did John restore anything? If so, why would Jesus have to come? It is true that, of John, Jesus said, "This is he of whom it is written, 'Behold, I send my messenger before thy face and he shall pre-pare the way before thee' " (Matt. 11:10, quoting Mal. 3:1). Christ emphatically stated that "Elijah is come already, and they knew him not. Then understood they that He spoke to them of John the Baptist" (Matt. 17:12-13), a misconception on their part because even after Christ's resurrection, the disciples were *still* asking, "Lord, dost thou at this time restore the kingdom to Israel?" (Acts 1:6). Therefore, since the Baptist did not restore "all things," he is not the personage referred to in Matthew 17:11.

However, John the Baptist, did come in the "power and spirit of Elijah," completely fulfilling Isaiah's description of the forerunner of the Messiah (40:3f). His conciliatory mission was intended to turn the hearts of a generation of disobedient, legalistic Jews to prepare them for the acceptance of the One whom their prophets had foretold (Mal. 4:6a). Otherwise, God would "come and smite the earth with a curse" (4:6b) — a divine judgment against the nation of Jews for rejecting His Christ, something emphatically fulfilled by Rome's conquest of Jerusalem in AD 70.

Chapter Four

DANIEL AND THE
KINGDOM OF GOD

T HE PREACHING and writing of Daniel is highly relevant to political and historical situations. Because of chapters 2 and 7–12, his book is also correctly classed as apocalyptic, a type of literature which was written in troublous times during periods of trial, sorrow and near despair. Amid the adversity, the prophet promised the faithful a time of deliverance from oppression and triumph over enemies.

The millennialist extracts portions of Daniel, and applies them far into the future, away from historical applications during 500 B.C. to AD 70, past nearly 2,000 years, to a yet-future earthly return of the Lord, who would *finally* preside over the long-awaited kingdom. To these theorists, the book of Daniel has end time references to the destruction of the Gentile world system which would exist during a "revived" Roman Empire, depicting it by an image of a statue as having toes long enough to reach to a yet-future "second coming" of Christ (Dan. 2:40-42).

This private rendering must be questioned in its very approach, because it ignores the immediate historical element, the closest possible fulfillment. By thus casting aside the principles of "by whom to whom," and of assigning primary application to contemporaries or perhaps subsequent generations, the premillennial interpretation offers little comfort and meaning to the faithful Jews of Daniel's day and others throughout the biblical era.

Any analysis of the book of Daniel surely must consider both its prophetical and historical contexts. Various millennial speculators concentrate on the former, and generally ignore the latter. In chapters 2 and 7, the prophet related the dynasties of an existing Babylonian nation and three successive future monarchies, the Babylonian, the Medo-Persian, and the Macedonian, ending with the "terrible and powerful and exceedingly strong" fourth beast (7:7), one which would smash – subdue – crush (2:40) and "devour the whole earth and break it into pieces" (7:23). This strong figure is the Roman Empire, as most commentators readily agree.

It would be in the days of those kings – before the depicted Romans finished their rule – that the God of Heaven would "set up" a kingdom (royal rule) which would never fail, one which would break and consume other kingdoms (2:44). Age-lasting, this spiritual kingdom would never be destroyed (7:14), and would rise permanently above all world kingdoms (see Isa. 2:2-5).

The One who would inherit the rule of this kingdom would be Jesus Christ. Daniel records His receiving this kingship from heaven's point of view: "And there was given Him [the Christ] dominion, and glory, and a kingdom, that all the peoples, nations and languages should serve Him: His dominion is an everlasting dominion . . ." (7:13-14). Psalm 2:8 prophetically announces the gift of this kingship from God to Christ: "Ask of me, and I will give thee the nations for thine inheritance." After Christ's ascension into heaven, where God crowned Him Lord and Christ, as Peter announced to his kinsmen on the Day of Pentecost that Jesus had been made "both Lord and Christ" – the King of kings (Acts 2:36). Thus, if God gave the kingdom to His Son during the time of the Roman Empire, Jesus is *now* king, a present reality. Paul wrote to the Colossians that God had transferred him and fellow saints into the kingdom of His beloved son (1:13; see also Rev. 19:6b).

The parable of the pounds (Luke 19:11-27) amplifies what Daniel had foretold. As the nobleman, Jesus went away to receive a kingdom and return. Earthly servants who had been given pounds to trade would have to give an account of themselves when the nobleman came back. Blessings would be bestowed according to faithfulness, in the same way that the Master issued additional talents to the productive servants in the parable of the talents (Matt. 25:14-30). But certain citizens, servants of the nobleman, would not allow their master to reign over them (v. 14). The nobleman then ordered the slaying of the unfaithful servants "that would not that I should reign over them" (v. 27).

This *reign* of Christ, and not a physical external entity over which He rules, is the focus of the kingdom. It is not an organization of earthly origin or power (John 18:36), but of the Master's rule over human hearts. The subjects constitute the body of Christ, the "New Testament church." Christ's dominion should always be defined in terms of kingship, royal power, and rule, and not by institutional or political standards.

On one occasion, a perceptive scribe said to Jesus that proper love with all the heart, understanding, and strength toward the one God and love of earthly neighbors was much more valuable than all whole offerings and sacrifices (Mark 12:32-33). In response, Jesus said, "You are not far from the kingdom of God." The nearness was in relation to the scribe's prudent, discreet response to Christ's teaching, and not near in a sense of a chronology involving a time of beginning. Jesus appreciated the scribe's state of mind, which showed that God could reign over his heart.

Christ's own announcement of the nearness of God's reign

is mentioned in Mark 1:15: "The time is fulfilled, and the kingdom of God is at hand [or nearby]." Jesus commissioned His disciples by telling them that as you go, proclaim that the kingdom of God is near (Luke 10:9). Jesus' public ministry told about the good news of the reign of God (Matt. 4:23, Luke 4:43). He would not have said that the kingdom is *near* if it were not to be made available for another few thousand years in the future.

The kingdom involves a pure heart and unqualified obedience to God. An affirmative response to the gospel would have allowed taxpayers and harlots entrance into the kingdom before the Pharisees (Matt. 21:31b-32). God's kingdom was certainly not in the hearts of most of the Pharisees whom Jesus met; in fact, the availability of God's reign would be removed from them (v. 43), because they had shut the kingdom of heaven against men (Matt. 23:13). Through indoctrination, various party leaders had tried to prevent many others from being subject to the reign. Paul declared to the Romans that the kingdom was characterized by righteousness, joy, and peace (14:7), as well as by obedience (Matt. 7:21).

When someone in a crowd of Jews asked Jesus when the kingdom of God would arrive, He replied that it did not come with observation, that is, in such a way that fleshly eyes could gaze upon it (Luke 17:20-21). The word "observation" uniquely appears here in the "New Testament," although variant forms of that verb in Luke denote the unfriendly manner in which the Pharisees observed the deeds of Jesus (6:7, 14:1, 20:20).

The essence of Jesus' answer is that the kingdom (reign) of God does not enter the hearts of men possessed with a hostile spirit. God's reign is no public spectacle wherein men can look and exclaim, "Lo, there it is!" Failing to see a spiritual application to the kingdom, the Pharisees did not perceive that the kingdom's essence was already in their midst – "within you" (Luke 17:21). "Within" is *entos,* as in "inside of the cup" (Matt. 23:26).

In the person of Christ, the kingdom was, at that moment, among them in the presence of the Son of man preaching in their very neighborhood, and only needed to be recognized. With all of their watching of Jesus, the Pharisees failed to understand the nature of the kingdom, but good hearts could seek it through faith, justice, and love. The kingdom is *not* a territory or a system of ecclesiastical machinery; in His preaching about God's reign, Jesus had a spiritual program in mind, a relationship with a Deliverer.

Some thought that the kingdom of God would immediately appear (Luke 19:11), but Jesus never limited its coming to a one-time occurrence, whether in the far future, at the so-called "second coming," or at Pentecost when the Holy Spirit came in Jesus' absence (John 16:7, 16-19). The latter is a strong example of fulfillment, as shown by Acts 2, Luke 22:18 and 24:46-49, and Daniel 2:44; but God's reign also begins (or is extended) any time a person becomes a penitent believer. He subjects his will to the King, entering His reign by an intellectual and moral change and a subsequent transformation of life. In that sense the kingdom "comes" to individuals today.

Therefore, the kingdom of God was meant to endure throughout the ages, increasing in its influence like Daniel's description of the stone cut from the mountain (2:34-36, 45), which itself "became a great mountain and filled the whole earth" (v.35). The kingdom would grow, and operate like the mustard seed and the leaven, until it accomplished its heavenly purpose among men. All teaching by Christ and the prophets concerning the kingdom contemplated a long time in which all anti-God authority and power would be subdued, "for He [Christ] must reign till He hath put all His enemies under His feet" (I Cor. 15:25).

The kingdom of God personified in Christ (Luke 21:31; compare carefully with Matt. 24:33) specifically "came" upon Jerusalem in AD 70, when Jesus displayed divine power by bringing judgment upon the disobedient, rebellious Jewish nation, while delivering the Christians to safety. The deliverance was by the warning given to messianic Jews to leave Judea, as recorded in Luke 21:31: "When you see this [signs] happening, you know that the kingdom of God is near," in the sense that His power would be displayed and His judgment faithfully carried out. Indeed, the overthrow of Jerusalem was among the first triumphs of the Messiah's reign, truly a demonstration that He was "seated at the right hand of power" (Matt. 26:64).

Thus, God's kingdom is not an end time physical nation to be established upon the earth, but it is wholly spiritual in both purpose and design, as Jesus Himself continuously preached. The kingdom is never limited geographically but is the royal rule of the Messiah in the hearts of believers. It is the *power* of the gospel to change a heart, so that Christ can reign over it.

This kingdom is not materialistic. It is not of an external source. It is "not of this world" (John 18:36). It is wholly spiritual, entered through reception of the covenant, received with humility (Luke 18:17), and peopled by obedient heaven-prepared subjects, who freely acknowledge Christ's kingship and allow Him to reign over their hearts. It is characterized by service: "Whosoever would become great among you shall be your minister" (Matt. 20:26).

Thus, as the Christ Himself now reigns, all faithful Christians, by the life and truth which they possess, also reign now through Him. Christians, in overcoming (Rev. 2:7, 3:21), enduring (II Tim. 2:11-12), and in their eating of the Lord's Supper, sit and reign with Christ in life (Rom. 5:17) "in the heavenly places" (Eph. 2:6). Christians are *now* a royal priesthood (I Pet. 2:9). Since Christ is presently our High Priest (Heb. 5:10, 6:20-8:3), He must also sit and rule upon His throne as King (Zech. 6:13).

Therefore, the prophetic announcements of the kingdom had their fulfillment in events associated with the first century saints in Christ. Clearly, the "law and the prophets were until John: from that time the gospel of the kingdom of God [Heaven's reign over hearts] is preached . . ." (Luke 16:16). The kingdom would not wait to be fulfilled in a premillennial reign, to commence far into the future during a revived Roman Empire, when temple sacrifices would be restored, along with the appearance of the end time antichrist. The latter is not any one individual, as the millennial speculators believe, but as the apostle John stated the antichrist is anyone who denies that Jesus came in the flesh as the Son of God. (I John 2:20, 4:3; II John 7).

Daniel 9: The Seventy Weeks

The prophet Daniel told of the course of future events that brought an end of the nation Israel in AD 70. These are discussed in two highly figurative passages, 9:24-27 and the entire Chapter 12. Both of Daniel's passages mention the "abomination of desolation," which Jesus definitely assigned to the time before the destruction of Jerusalem (Matt. 24:15, Mark 13:14). This ascription by Jesus Himself is therefore not subject to human reservation or a partial fulfillment.

The vision of the Seventy weeks and the anointed prince (9:24-27) is an oft-used premillennial passage:

(24) Seventy weeks are decreed upon thy people and upon thy holy city, to finish transgression, and to make an end of sins, and to make reconciliation for iniquity, and to bring in everlasting righteousness, and to seal up vision and prophecy, and to anoint the most holy. (25) Know therefore and discern, that from the going forth of the commandment to restore and to build Jerusalem unto the anointed one, the prince, shall be seven weeks, and threescore and two weeks: it shall be built again, with street and moat, even in troublous times. (26) And after the threescore and two weeks shall the anointed one be cut off and shall have nothing: and the people of the prince that shall come shall destroy the city and the sanctuary; and the end thereof shall be with a flood, and even unto the end shall be war; desolations are determined. (27) And he shall make a firm covenant with many for one

week: and in the midst of the week he shall cause the sacrifice and the oblation to cease; and upon the wing of abominations shall come one that maketh desolate: and even unto the full end, and that determined, shall wrath be poured out upon the desolate.

The familiar "a day equals a year" millennial interpretation of the above material means that the seventy weeks would extend over a literal 490 year period. Various expositors widely differ as to when this period begins and ends, and the juggling of historical facts to fit the 490 years shows the fallacy of such assumptions. The seventy sevens more likely represents an indefinite complete fullness of time, perhaps symbolic of the seventy year captivity. When Jesus said to forgive "seventy times seven" (Matt. 18:22), He obviously had in mind an indefinite number of times.

Six statements in verse 24 describe the Messiah and what He would do; all were fulfilled with His mission and work on earth. The oft-debated verse 25 mentions the event which initiated the seventy weeks "decreed upon thy people" (v. 24a). This was the "going forth of the commandment to restore and to build Jerusalem." Likely the decree of Cyrus in 536 B.C. to rebuild Jerusalem is meant, though more than a dozen major interpretations exist, each with its own year as a starting point! (see Edward Beiderwolf, The *Second Coming Bible* pp. 216-225). There should not be so much concern over a beginning or an ending as over the substance and purpose of the passage.

The first seven weeks likely extend to Ezra in 432 B.C., when the city walls were rebuilt. The period of 62 weeks mentioned in verse 26a is probably the era of about 450 years between Malachi and Christ, reaching to the time when the anointed One would be "cut off" (v. 26b), that is, at the cross. The difficult verse 27 declares that a covenant would be made with many for one week and that sacrifices would cease, and then abominations and desolations would appear when wrath would be poured out.

The week in verse 27 is the last of three time segments in

the vision. If the first prophetic time period of "seven weeks" was fulfilled in 104 literal years, and the second period of "62 weeks" spans about 450 literal years, then the final "one week" should consistently be a literal time period of less than seven weeks, just as the 62 weeks is more than the seven weeks.

The 37-year period between the cross of Christ and the Roman destruction of Jerusalem in AD 70 fits neatly as the terminus of the third time period of Daniel's "one week." That the weeks and years of the three time periods are not strictly proportionate does not matter, for Daniel was primarily concerned with relating a sequence of events rather than fixing precise corresponding dates to fit a numerical calculation. Any effort to pursue the latter always encounters immense difficulties.

Verse 27 also declares that there would be a "full end upon the desolate." This judgment would come upon "thy people . . . and thy holy city" (v. 24), the subject of the phrase in verse 27. God's wrath would be poured out upon the "desolate," the very word Jesus used when He contemplated the fall of Jerusalem in Matthew 23:38: "Your house is left unto you *desolate*." The next several verses of Matthew extending into Chapter 24 lead to Jesus' reference to the "abomination of desolation, which was spoken of through Daniel the prophet . . . " (Matt. 24:15). Therefore, Jesus' comment on the desolate city and His reference to Daniel's "wing of abominations that maketh desolate" should leave little doubt that the seventieth week terminates with the destruction of Jerusalem by General Titus and his legions in AD 70.

The "people of the prince" (v. 26) were likely the Roman soldiers with their general who destroyed the city and the sanctuary, as mentioned in the middle of the verse. The "flood" was an overflowing of destroying invaders, identical to the Assyrians' sweeping and overflowing Judea in about 720 B.C., as described by Isaiah, reaching to the very neck of the nation, Jerusalem itself (8:8). In 9:26, Daniel employed the same figure. The desolations that are determined are realized at the end of verse 27.

The middle of verse 27 mentions that the sacrifice and meal offerings would cease, in the midst of (or during) the week. This event likely refers to the cessation of temple sacrifices just before the "full end." The "wing of abominations" were sacriligious acts in the temple; the "wing" is literally "pinnacle" or roof. If the pinnacle is a synecdoche for the temple, an amplified reading of that verse would be: "On the roof of the temple shall come the abominations of the one what maketh desolate." The "wrath" is Christ executing vengeance through the Romans armies upon the desolate people, bringing the Jewish apostates to a "full end," but not the entire race (Jer. 30:11, 46:28).

Therefore, Daniel's seventy weeks extend from the time of Cyrus (536 B.C.) past the rebuilding of Solomon's temple into the gospel era and the death of the Christ, the initiation of His reign, the ending of temple service, and the coming of the Prince who would terminate the Jewish state in AD 70. Nothing is left to be fulfilled.

Daniel 12: The Time of the End

Throughout Daniel chapter 12, the author tells of events leading to the fall of Jerusalem in AD 70, and not to the yet-future final return of Christ, for verse 11 mentions the "abomination that maketh desolate [that would be] set up." (Another occurrence of this phrase is at 11:31, where it probably refers to Antiochus Epiphanes, who also profaned the temple sanctuary in about 165 B.C.)

The unprecedented misery and suffering, "There shall be a time of trouble, such as never was since there was a nation even to that same time . . . " (v. 1) unmistakably corresponds to Matthew's "great tribulation" (24:21). "Many of them that sleep in the dust of the earth shall awake . . . " (v. 2) does not refer to the end time bodily resurrection because then *all* shall awake. It is a figurative resurrection of a cause, just as in Ezekiel 37:12, where Jewish saints were resurrected for a cause symbolic of the return from Babylonian captivity. Therefore, verses 1-3 closely correspond to the time preceding Jerusalem's fall, where covenant people through Christ triumphed over unfaithful Jews.

In verse 7, the "breaking in pieces the power of the holy people" occurred in AD 70, when "all these things" would be finished (v. 7b; compare with Matt. 24:3, 34). The "time of the end" in both verses 4 and 9 directly refers to the destruction of the Hebrew commonwealth. The "they that are wise shall understand" (v. 10) would have complete revelation and insight to escape from the city (compare with Joel 2:32) prior to the end, but "none of the wicked shall understand" and thus they would perish in the siege of Jerusalem. Jesus provided the clue to begin preparation for flight in the "abomination that maketh desolate," for that sign plainly appeared in prelude to the fall of the city in AD 70.

Thus, Daniel 12 is a description of the divine presence of Jesus Christ coming with His holy ones upon the nation Israel, destroying the city of Jerusalem, using His human instrument the Roman armies. The end of the Jewish state therefore occurred precisely as the "law, the prophets and the Psalms" had foretold. Though Isaiah, Jeremiah, David and Moses generally told of the destruction, Joel, Malachi and Daniel specified people and events which would be associated with the era before the fall of Jerusalem.

Joel wrote that the Holy Spirit would come on the Pentecost of Acts 2, at the onset of the generation before "the great and terrible day of Jehovah," the destruction of Jerusalem (2:28-32). Before that same day, Malachi prophesied of the arrival of "Elijah," Jesus the Christ (4:5). Daniel foretold the "abomination of desolation" which Jesus would specifically relate to the time before the same destruction (Matt. 24:15). These references are sure and settled from which there should be no appeal, for personages and authors in the New Testament are commenting on long-familiar Jewish writings and declaring that they have been fulfilled.

Summary

The Jewish prophets long taught that the kingdom is Yahweh's, and that He is ruler among the nations (Psa. 22:28). "Say among the nations, Yahweh reigneth . . . He will judge the peoples with equity . . . He cometh to judge the earth: He will judge the world in righteousness, and the peoples with His truth" (Psa. 96:10-13).

Ever since the Pentecost of Acts 2, this office (work) of dispensing righteous judgment and magnifying goodness has rested in the person of Jesus Christ (Rev. 1:5, 12:5, 17:14, 19:16). The Father has given Him "authority to execute judgment because He is a Son of man" (John 5:27). He now reigns from His glorious throne situated at His father's right hand. (Acts 2:30-36), guarding the hearts of His covenanted ones.

In various signs and wonders throughout the first century gospel era, Jesus manifested His power. In the destruction of Jerusalem and its temple, He came in judgment against Jewish people who had perverted the kingdom and their covenant with God. In execution, He functioned as a reigning king, and so His kingship did not begin at the time of the destruction of Jerusalem or in a millennium preceding the yet future "second coming."

Paul wrote that Jesus would continue to reign until all enemies were under His feet and then would deliver the kingdom to the Father, as part of His royal rule (I Cor. 15:24). On that day of the general resurrection, the "end (v. 25)," death and hades would be destroyed forever (I Cor. 15:26, John 5:28-29, Rev. 20:14). In a most impressive parabolic scene of the end time judgment, Matthew shows how King Jesus would judge the living and the dead, separating sheep from goats (25:31-46).

Chapter Five

THE DESTRUCTION OF JERUSALEM
IN THE SYNOPTIC GOSPELS

A LL THREE of the synoptic gospels – Matthew, Mark, and Luke – contain ominous references to judgment upon first century Jerusalem. In the wilderness of Judea, just before Jesus began His own ministry among the lost sheep of the house of Israel, John the Baptist was preaching repentance, "for the kingdom of heaven is at hand" (Matt. 3:2). When many among the Pharisees and Sadducees had come to the Jordan River to critically appraise his actions, John, in noting their evil motives, exclaimed, "Ye generation of vipers, who has warned you to flee from the wrath to come?" (v. 7). These men, full of guile and malice, had no good reason to come to John, only to spy on him. The "wrath to come" was God's destruction of Jerusalem in AD 70, something which those very party-centered Jews would experience.

Matthew 3:11-12 presents an even more striking figure of divine vengeance to be meted upon the once-favored nation. The Jews would be metaphorically baptized in fire, which is a destruction of the wicked. In verse 12 Christ holds a winnowing fan, a fork-like tool used to separate the valuable wheat from the lighter chaff, which freely blew away when both were tossed into the wind. A fan, an instrument of judgment, held in His hand meant that, even at the time Jesus came to be baptized of John, the dutiful process of sifting evil Jews from the righteous ones already had begun. Therefore, a part of Christ's earthly mission included bringing judgment against the Israel of His generation.

When Jesus in the Limited Commission ordered the twelve to "go to the lost sheep of Israel" (Matt. 10:5f), He declared that they "shall not have gone through the cities of Israel, till the Son of man be come" (v. 23). This "coming" involves Jesus' providential presence in the Roman armies as they overwhelmed the Jewish nation. Even in this initial commission, the apostles were not to tarry in cities which would not receive them. Christ promised that for them "it shall be more tolerable for the land of Sodom and Gomorrah in the day of judgment, than for that city" (v. 15).

Thus, the apostles themselves would not evangelize all of Judea's cities before Christ's visitation of Jerusalem in judgment a generation after the cross. Luke adds, "If the mighty works had been done in Tyre and Sidon [non-Jewish cities] which were done in you, they would have repented long ago" (10:13). Jesus uttered this statement in response to the cool reception to the preaching of the kingdom of God in Capernaeum, Bethsaida, and Chorazin, three Jewish cities immediately northwest of the Sea of Galilee.

Jesus knew where to find His lost sheep among Israel. Perhaps the Master contemplated Jeremiah's statement: "Hear the word of Jehovah, O ye nations and declare it in the isles afar off; and say, He that scattereth Israel will gather him, and keep him, as a shepherd doth his flock" (31:10). The ancient prophet was explaining to God's covenant people the grandeur of the blessings which they would receive upon their return from Babylonian captivity, in 536 B.C. These spiritual promises would again be realized in the time of Christ, but the contemporary Jews rejected Him, and so they were as "sheep" to be slaughtered during the time of the capture of Jerusalem in AD 70.

In Matthew 9:12-13 the Pharisees noted that Jesus was dining with the tax collectors, people who were deemed sinners. The Master defended His conduct with a proverb: "they that are whole have no need of a physician, but they that are sick." At that time, the spiritually ill nation of Israel needed a restoration of spiritual health through "dosages" of how to maintain its covenant relationship with God, through the teaching of the gospel of Christ. In another context, Jesus unequivocally called them "dead" (Matt. 8:22).

"Some that Stand by Here . . ." – Mark 8:38-9:1

A particularly often misunderstood verse, Mark 8:38-9:1 relates important truths about Christ coming in His kingdom. "Verily I say unto you, there are some here of them that stand by, who shall by no means taste of death, till they see the kingdom of God come with power." The parallel in Matthew 16:28 reads ". . . till they see the Son of man coming in his kingdom." Luke simply expresses it as ". . . till they see the kingdom of God" (9:27). These declarations were probably oft repeated during Jesus' ministry.

The phrase, "some that stand by here . . . ." clearly references the disciples and others about Him. In saying "some," the verse very likely presupposes that the majority of the people Jesus addressed would have died before the event in question – the coming of the Son of man in the kingdom with power. This statement was uttered only six days before His transfiguration, so fulfillment is neither in that event or in the crucifixion nor resurrection eight months later.

That only "some" will not have died implies a more distant event, one further into the future than the several months to the Pentecost of Acts 2. Moreover, Mark 9:1 is silent about the demonstration of the Spirit through the apostles or the power of gospel preaching associated with that first Pentecost. Conversely, Acts 2 says nothing about fulfillment of the coming of the kingdom with power or that the Christ "came" on that day.

Fulfillment must have come much later, for without a doubt practically all (and not merely just *some*) in the audience were still living at that Pentecost. For a Pentecost fulfillment, it must be assumed that the "power" was the arrival of the Holy Spirit (but Jesus who is to come is *one* person, and the Holy Spirit is *"another* comforter" (John 14:16), and the word "some" must be rendered to convey the idea of "many" or "most."

Other occurrences of "some" in Mark refer to a minority, as at 4:4–7: "some seed fell by the wayside . . . some seed fell on stony places . . . other fell among the thorns." Some (not most) of the disciples ate with unwashed hands (7:2). In asking "Who do men say that I am?" Jesus was told that "some say that thou are John the Baptist. . . " (8:28). In Simon's house, "some had indignation among themselves" (14:4). As Jesus appeared before the high priest prior to His crucifixion, "some began to spit on Him . . ." (14:65). At His cross "some of them that stood by" said that Jesus called for Elijah (15:35); carefully note the nearly identical construction of that verse with the one under discussion, 9:1. In each of these cases, far less than a majority are contemplated by the word "some." It would thus appear that the word "some" of Mark 9:1 sets apart a minority of the group in question.

In view of the context, the destruction of Jerusalem, almost forty years into the future, adequately fulfills the truths stated in Mark 8:38–9:1. The time also harmonizes well with Mark 13:30 and Matthew 24:34, both of which declare that Christ's generation would not pass until the famines, the false christs, the earthquakes, and all the other things mentioned in those contexts would be accomplished. Jesus did come in power at the termination of the Jewish nation, revealing messianic glory and demonstrating His kingship and rule over the nations.

Parallel to Mark 8:38-9:1 is Mark 13:26-27, 30. Six common phrases occur in both passages. Each uses the words "Son of man," "coming," "glory," and "angels." The phrase "adulterous and sinful generation" of 8:38 precisely coincides with "this generation shall not pass" of 13:30. The latter also is parallel to Mark 9:1: "there are some here of them that stand by who in no wise shall taste of death. . . . " Mark 9:1 uses the phrase "kingdom of God come;" 13:29 says "he [it] is nigh," but the "it" is the kingdom of God according to Luke 21:31. Since Mark 13 is undeniably a discourse on the destruction of Jerusalem, Mark 8:38-9:1 must also refer to the same event.

Thus reinforced by Mark 13:26-27, 30, the difficult passage Mark 8:38-9:1 best refers to the manifestation of Jesus as the victorious King, at the time when religiously and socially corrupt Judaism was overturned by Rome in AD 70. Men who were "standing by" in Mark 9:1 did witness the beginning of the end (Pentecost), the extension of the kingdom with power (throughout Acts), and "some of them" (Mark 9:1) did live until the fall of Jerusalem in the year 70 to witness firsthand the removing of the disloyal Jewish candlestick from its place.

At another time, Jesus enjoined watchfulness and readiness by admonishing the disciples to be in constant expectation of Christ's coming. "Let your loins be girded about, and let your lamps burning; and be ye yourselves like unto men looking for their lord, when he shall return from the marriage feast; that, when he cometh and knocketh, they may straightway open unto him . . . Blessed are those servants, whom the Lord when he cometh shall find watching . . . Be ye also ready: for in an hour that ye think not, the Son of man cometh" (Luke 12:35-40). These people already had been given the kingdom (v. 32), but they had to keep their lamps burning in readiness for the Master's impending return. The tribulation which came upon

Jerusalem came suddenly and unexpectedly to the unprepared. See also Mark 13:33-37.

Luke 12:49 declares that Christ came to cast fire upon the earth, an expression which likely refers to the mid-first century random conflict and persecution which followed the preaching of Christ's gospel. It aroused the opposition of orthodox institutional Jews. In standing against Christ, they would perish when the city fell. During His ministry, Jesus brought division to families (v. 51). The parallel in Matthew 10:34 mentions that He brought a sword, a symbol of war. Since the persecutors used it upon the Christians, Jesus would turn it against these same Jews when Rome came upon Jerusalem to destroy it in AD 70.

Luke 12:58-59 contains still another admonition for the nation to repent: "For as thou art going with thine adversary before the magistrate, on the way give diligence to be quit of him; lest haply he drag thee unto the judge, and the judge shall deliver thee to the officer, and the officer shall cast thee into prison. I say unto thee, thou shalt by no means come out thence, till thou have paid the very last mite." Anyone hearing these words should have the wisdom to come to terms with an adversary before being taken into court, where the judge would turn him over to the officer, who would cast him into prison (v. 58b). The prisoner could not be released until he had paid his debt.

The lesson to visible Israel, if wise, was that the nation had to turn to God while there was still time. It is essential to seek peace with God before the day of grace and mercy passes. Early in the first century, the course which Jewish partisans were taking could only result in a head-on collision with the Romans and consequent disaster. Repentance, a turning to Christ, would have prevented the fall of the nation. Since the Jews did not act while they were still able to do so, they would meet destruction in the year AD 70 by the power of Christ through the instrument the Roman armies.

Luke 18:1-8 tells about an unrighteous judge and a God-fearing widow. Though she received no help from him initially, the judge finally gave her legal protection (v. 5). God in contrast would speedily avenge His elect who continue in prayer (v. 7). In view of God's faithfulness, Jesus asked, "Nevertheless, when the Son of man cometh, shall he find the faith on the earth?" (v. 8). Stated simply, would the disciples still pray (v. 1) and abide in the faith? Or would they apostatize, by failing to stand up against severe persecution by unrighteous Jews during the years before the destruction of Jerusalem? The saints had to acquire the deep faith which the widow possessed, and the assurance that God is a righteous Judge. Jesus demonstrated His Judgeship by coming in righteous vengeance upon the apostate Jews that had refused Him.

Concerning the Israelite nation, the Lord also said, "The Son of man is come to seek and to save that which was lost" (Luke 19:10). Jesus repeated the very words which Ezekiel had used 600 years before, in reference to apostate Judah. On that earlier occasion, God said that "I will feed my flock, and I will cause them to lie down, saith Yahweh. I will seek that which was lost" (34:16).

In both cases God had provided a way of deliverance for His people. The Jewish parties contemporary with Christ rejected His teaching of restoration and covenant and thus they would see their end in AD 70, just as Judah in Ezekiel's day met destruction in 586 B.C.

The Parable of the Pounds

In the Parable of the Pounds (Luke 19:11-27), the servants were given talents for trading purposes until the nobleman (Jesus) would come. The servants, both Jewish and Gentile Christians, had to give an account of themselves (v. 15b); existing alongside them were the citizens. But the latter hated the nobleman, and sent an assemblage after him, saying, "We will not let this man reign over us" (v. 14).

These rebellious Jews refused the Christ's rule as king. After the servants gave an account of their trading, Jesus said, "But these mine enemies, that would not that I should reign over them, bring hither, and slay them before me" (v. 27).

For failing to allow Christ to rule over their hearts, the rebellious citizens would experience the terrible punishment which befell Jerusalem in the year 70. These stiff-necked Jews failed to acknowledge His kingship and universal rule. They were enemies who killed and persecuted good hearts who followed the way of the cross. Their end was death, and in fact they were slain before Christ in the fall of Jerusalem.

The Parable of the Two Sons

In the Parable of the Two Sons (Matt. 21:28-31), one of them was asked by his father to work on a certain day in the vineyard. This son chose not to go, but later changed his mind and went. The second said that he would enter the field but did not do so. In response to Jesus' question about which son did the will of the father, the chief priests, scribes, and elders said, "The first."

They responded correctly. But the first son stood for the "publicans and harlots" who would go into the kingdom of God before those same Jewish leaders. The publicans and harlots did make a step toward God's way by believing in John's (v. 32). Though imperfect, their attitude was far better than the unfaithful Israelites and Jews, embodied in the second son.

These had been commissioned by the Father, the vineyard owner, to bring forth a cash crop. They said that they would labor in the vineyard but failed to show for work. These chief priests, scribes and elders were saturated with the misconception that they were still faithful before God. But continual disobedience led to their dismissal from God's vineyard. The audience did not perceive the disguise of the parable – that it was aimed at them.

The Parable of the Husbandmen

While His audience was still speculating on the identity of the two sons, Jesus thrust upon them a parable involving a wicked husbandmen (Matt. 21:33-45, Mark 12:1-12, Luke 20:9-19). In it, God removed His favor from wicked Jews because of their ingratitude and their sinfulness and gave it to the Gentiles and reformed Jews who once again enjoyed God's covenant (Rom. 11:13-25). In relating this story, Jesus paraphrased another similar parable, with which His audience was familiar, Isaiah 5:1-7. The nation of Israel is clearly the vineyard in each parable.

A householder leased his vineyard to husbandmen who developed the property. But when the owner sent servants to collect the rent from the husbandmen, they beat them, stoned them and even killed them. Finally, the householder sent his only son, his last resource, to see if any gratitude were left (v. 37). But the husbandmen thought only of killing him and cast him out of the vineyard to fulfill their deed.

The householder is God. The vineyard is the house of Israel which God had planted in Palestine. He had hedged about it (separated Israel from the other nations), protected it, and dug a winepress in its midst – that is, He had given it divine sanction. He also built a tower, thus establishing the royal house of David.

The husbandmen represent the ruling religious class of institutional Israel – the Pharisees and other parties, chief priests, elders, etc. – and the son is Christ. The servants are God's messengers and prophets sent to Israel from time to time to bring the people to Him (II Kgs. 17:13). Some were martyrs: Jeremiah was stoned according to tradition, and other prophets were beaten, knifed. and sawn asunder (I Kgs. 19:10; II Chron. 24:20-21, 36:16; Heb. 11:36-37). This long line of servants ended with John the Baptist, whose murder only a year or two before was still fresh in their minds.

These Jewish partisans knew that, in the son, Jesus was referring to Himself, so they listened attentively for Him to make some mistake for which they could lay their hands on Him. Instead, the Jews now heard their own fate unfold before them, as Jesus uttered boldly the words which heretofore had only been whispered about in the temple precincts. Jesus calmly proceeded with the climax of the story about the husbandmen: "And they caught him, and cast him out of the vineyard, and slew him" (Matt. 21:39).

Jesus next related the consequences of the action of the wicked Jews in putting the son to death: "When the Lord of the vineyard cometh, what will He do?" The leaders' reply was that the miserable husbandmen were worthy of destruction. They further said that the land should then be leased to other tenants who would be able to remit the royalties on time, paying the proceeds at the proper season (v. 41).

Having secured the desired answer, Jesus challenged the chief priests, scribes and elders with another question: "Did you not read in the scriptures, 'The stone which the builders rejected, The same is become the head of the corner; This was from the Lord, And it is marvellous in our eyes?' " (v. 42). In this quotation from Psalm 118:22, the builders are the Jewish leaders, and the stone is the Christ, who would become the cornerstone of His *ekklesia*, the assembly of called-out saints (Matt. 16:18, I Cor. 3:11).

The change of language is abrupt and violent. It is unintelligible without a familiarity with metaphor and simile. In facing the hostile crowd, Jesus moved from the figure of the cornerstone back to plain words: "The kingdom of God shall be taken from you and given to a nation bringing forth the fruits thereof" (Matt. 21:43) – a holy nation (I Pet. 2:7-10). The change in state would be in favor of righteous Gentiles (Rom. 10:19, 11:25) and repentant Jews who were regrafted onto salvation's olive tree (Rom. 11:24).

This direct statement hit the Jewish leaders like a stinging fist. With the authority of a prophet, Jesus threatened their re-

ligious and political position by declaring that the Jewish nation was like the son in the previous parable who said that he
would work in the vineyard but did not go (Matt. 21:29).

Jesus continued, "And he that falleth on this stone shall be
broken to pieces: but on whomsoever it shall fall, it will scatter
him as dust" (Matt. 21:44). The first of the two fates upon
those Jews occurred in their conflict with Jesus; by falling on
Him they would merely be "broken" – such as by fracture of
some of their limbs. Whosoever fell upon the Christ stumbled
upon Him as a "rock of offense" (I Pet. 2:6-8, Matt. 11:6, Isa.
8:14-15). Though "broken," those afflicted would not be utterly destroyed.

But in the second act, when the stone would fall upon
them, because of rejecting Him as the stone for the corner of
their spiritual house, institutional rabbinic Judaism would be
ground and scattered as dust. Literally, they would be win-
nowed. In Daniel 2:35, pieces of the broken image on a
summer threshing floor collected like chaff which the wind
would carry away. Similarly, the unregenerate Jews would be
thrown off like husks of grain from the winnowing fan.

Jesus leaves no doubt of their depravity. Historically, the
Jewish nation had not been faithful to the Rock of Israel
(Deut. 32:15, 18, 30; Psa. 19:14; II Sam. 22:32, 23:2-3). They
also knew of Daniel's interpretation of the rock which would
grind to powder the kingdoms of Babylonian succession. They
were well aware that Jesus claimed to be the son of God. And
most especially, these degenerates realized that He is telling
them that they are severely out of favor and have already been
rejected by God and could never be exalted in the kingdom
unless they turned to Christ (Matt. 21:45). These Jewish leaders were not about to do such a thing. Thus, Christ would
bring to bear His power upon those rebellious Jews in judgment, something which would occur in that very generation
which ended with the fall of Jerusalem in the year 70. The
ruin would be deplorable beyond any similar event.

In Matthew's next story, the parable of the wedding feast

(22:1-14), God arranged a marriage for His son. Several servants, including the prophets, John the Baptist, and various disciples invited all kinds of Jews to the feast. Later other servants were sent forth – apostles, evangelists, other Christians. Not only did these Jews refuse both invitations, but some treated the servants disgracefully and killed them.

These things saw fulfillment in the persecution of the apostles and other early saints in Christ by fanatical Jews, as shown in Acts 4:3; 5:18, 40; 7:58; 8:3 and elsewhere. When the king heard what had happened, he was incensed and sent forth His armies to destroy those murderers and their city (Matt. 22:7). To inflict the retribution upon the citizens of Jerusalem, God, through the Christ, used Rome as the instrument of their fate. Verse 9, "go ye therefore into the highways," shows that all peoples would be invited, a fulfillment realized when the gospel was extended to the Gentiles.

Earlier events that transpired during the course of Jesus' triumphal entry into Jerusalem have overtones pointing to the decadence of Israel. The healing of blind Bartimaeus (Mark. 10:46-52), a man of great faith who wanted only to follow Jesus into Jerusalem, stands in bold contrast to the blindness of the party leaders of Israel, whose eyes remained sealed to the glory of Jesus.

Jesus' humble entry into Jerusalem on the lowly donkey (Luke 19:29-40), instead of in glory on the clouds of heaven, or on a great and strong military horse, or even on foot astride the other pilgrims, is an overt declaration of Israel's unworthiness. Jesus' mount fulfills Zechariah 9:9-10 and affirms His kingship and rule from "sea to sea." This symbolic act pointed to impending judgment.

The incident about the unproductive fig tree (Mark 11:12-14, 20-22) involves a prophetic warning of the terrible fate that would come upon a rebellious people. Jesus saw an ownerless fig tree full of leaves but without fruit growing on it. The grand display of foliage was nothing but empty pretense, just as after the mid-first century the glorious temple of gold and marble and its ceremony lacked the presence of God-fearing people. Jesus cursed the tree and it soon withered, indicating that judgment awaited Jerusalem soon.

Israel had not brought forth the fruit of righteousness required by God. "Withered from the roots . . . " indicates totality of destruction" (Hos. 9:16, Ezek. 17:9). Several Jewish prophets employed the fig tree to symbolize Israel's positive status before Yahweh (Jer. 8:13, 29:17; Mic. 7:1; Joel 1:7, 12; Hos. 9:10, 16).

Destruction of the tree pointed to the judgment of the nation (Hos. 2:12, Isa. 34:4). In Luke 13:6-9, the institutional temple cult is pictured as an unproductive three-year-old fig tree, but Israel would be given one more season to bear fruit before it would have to be hewn down. Truly, Judaism was already in its "fourth year" and the nation would have to show its worth or be cut from God's redeemed.

In the middle of the fig tree incident is Jesus in holy, fiery indignation (Mal.3:2-3) expelling the merchants from the temple precincts (Mark 11:15-17). These two stories mutually comment on judgment upon the nation.

Jesus cleansed the temple because the Jewish religious party leaders had allowed the court to be a refuge for robbers and a mart for exchangers and dove peddlers. In response, Jesus cited Jeremiah 7:10-11, in which Nebuchadnezzar of Babylon is seen as God's punisher of rebellious Judah prior to Jerusalem's destruction in 586 B.C.

The failure of temple authorities to respect the sanctity of the outer courts created the climate which allowed the temple to be taken over by sacrilegious Zealots in the year 68 and led to the city's ruin very shortly thereafter. God's spiritual house would then be a restored house of prayer for all nations (Isa. 56:7). But Jesus' boldness in the temple aroused the hostility of the chief priests, who thereafter sought a way to destroy Him.

The Generation of Jews in Jesus' Day

A tracing of the word "generation" throughout the New Testament emphasizes the depths of degradation and the baseness of the orthodox Jews contemporary with Christ and the apostles. They were unbelieving and difficult. Jesus cried, "O faithless and perverse generation, how long shall I be with you? How shall I bear with you?" (Matt. 17:17, Mark 9:19, Luke 9:41). The constant manifestation of little faith by these Jews made Jesus weary and sad.

The generation was fundamentally untrue to God and indistinguishable from the unregenerate. On Pentecost Simon Peter admonished his audience to "save yourselves from this perverse generation" (Acts 2:40). Paul wrote years later, within a decade of the fall of Jerusalem, that amidst a "crooked and perverse generation" the people of Christ were to be lights to the world, blameless and harmless (Phil. 2:15).

"How could I liken this generation?" Jesus on one occasion asked rhetorically (Matt. 11:16-19, Luke 7:31-35). It was like obstinate children playing in the public places. Jesus was comparing capricious juveniles with the contemporary Jewish party leaders who were dissatisfied at the preaching and lifestyles of both Jesus and John the Baptist. They had seen many miracles and had heard the gospel of the kingdom preached but knowingly failed to believe in Christ. The sins in the Gentile cities of Tyre and Sidon would be tolerated more in the day of judgment than that generation of wayward Jews (Matt. 11:22).

Being evil, they could not speak good things, and Christ forcefully addressed them as guileful and hypocritical. They were an offspring of vipers (Matt. 12:34), just as John the Baptist had said (Matt. 3:7, Luke 3:7). That unfaithful generation sought a sign (Matt. 12:39, 16:4), thus rendering useless all of His work. They were "adulterous and sinful," an expression related to Isaiah's in denouncing the perverseness of Judah in about 740 B.C. (1:4, 21).

Thus, Jesus would be ashamed of them when He came in the glory of His father with His holy angels (Mark 8:38). Ninevah, which had turned to God, would rise in judgment against this unrepentant generation of Jewish party leaders and condemn it (Matt. 12:41; see also Luke 11:32). Even the "Queen of the south" (Arabia?) praised God (v. 42); she would therefore "rise up in the judgment with this generation."

In still another parable, Jesus likened the Jews whom He met to a mad man with seven evil spirits in him (Matt. 12:43-45). Initially, he harbored but one which had been cast out during a time of transient repentance. Jesus warned that the spirits would return to the unregenerate. When the man again relapsed into sin, the evil spirit came back, bringing along seven others equally vile.

Formal Judaism as practiced during the generation after the crucifixion perfectly illustrates how spirits would return to dwell within the impenitent. Throughout the first century gospel era, those Jews became even more impious than those whom Jesus had encountered. The continually increasing wickedness and rejection of the gospel culminated in the five years of dreadful events associated with the destruction of Jerusalem. By AD 70, the last state of these partisans was indeed far worse than the first.

In an interesting exchange, the Pharisees and Sadducees tested Jesus by asking Him to show them a sign from heaven. Jesus answered them by saying, "When it is evening, ye say it will be fair weather: for the heaven is red. And in the morning, it will be foul weather today: for the heaven is red and lowering. Ye know how to discern the face of the heaven; but ye cannot discern the sign of the times" (Matt 16:1-4; see also Mark 8:11f).

Jesus noted that these hypocritical religious power leaders could read the meaning of common signs for weather forecasting, but they could not discern the spiritual events transpiring before their very eyes, that Christ would suffer, rise again, provide His followers with power to preach the gospel, and come in His kingdom in judgment against them. All of these things were as plain as sunshine and showers, but these men failed to perceive the meaning of Christ's teachings (see also Luke 11:29-30, 12:54-56).

Jesus concluded the discourse by saying that "an evil and adulterous generation seeks after a sign" (Matt. 16:1-4). They were evil because they sought to destroy Him and were adulterous, or unfaithful, because they embraced manufactured traditions and doctrines thought to be based on the Torah (Matt. 15:9), while holding to a mere semblance of the weighty matters of God's law (Matt. 23:23). Plainly, Jesus was confronting corrupt people claiming to be authentic Israel. Many among the Pharisees, the most guilty of distorting God's covenantal religion, were destined for the damnation of hell (Matt. 23:33).

Throughout Matthew 23, Jesus bitterly denounced the scribes and Pharisees in their quest for public recognition and their human-devised ritualism. These "separatists" were arrogant pretenders, blind guides, fools, guilty of all kinds of extortion and excess, were inwardly full of iniquity and hypocrisy, and were unclean as if full of dead men's bones. They had garnished the tombs of the righteous, shutting up the kingdom of heaven against men. All of their proselytes were twice the sons of hell as they were themselves. The Pharisees essentially had not changed since the days of John the Baptist, who had told them, "Who hath warned you to flee from the wrath to come?" (Luke 3:7). Jesus said in similar fashion, "How can ye escape the judgement of hell?" (Matt. 23:33).

In Matthew 23:34-39 (Luke 11:49-51), Jesus delivered another severe charge to contemporary Talmudic Judaism and laments over the city which God had always shown much love and tenderness. Jesus would send teachers and apostles who would be murdered by unrepentant Jews during the gospel era after the cross. He climaxed His speech with this startling statement: "Upon you may come all the righteous blood shed on earth, from the blood of right-hearted Abel unto the blood of Zechariah . . . whom ye slew between the sanctuary and the altar. Verily I say unto you, all these things shall come upon this generation" (v. 36).

As the Amorites were not punished until their iniquity was full (Gen. 15:16), so the transgressions of Jewish degenerates were allowed to accumulate over the centuries until the generation of Christ. Throughout history these leaders maintained a tradition of adding to the previous murders of God's messengers, and now Jesus was addressing the generation which would be held accountable for all past evil deeds, climaxing with the miracles of the apostles and prophets sent to them (see Matt. 23:34). But God would not let the deed go unnoticed. Within a generation, by AD 70, the collected vengeance broke upon the Jews in the unparalleled sufferings in the siege and collapse of Jerusalem.

Yet, with infinite tenderness, Jesus in His last public address mourned the city: "O Jerusalem, Jerusalem, that killeth the prophets, and stoneth them that are sent unto her! How often would I have gathered thy children together, even as a hen gathereth her chickens under her wings and ye would not!" (Matt. 23:37, Luke 13:34). Had these Jews repented, Jesus would have provided them the closeness of maternal protection, even as a hen hovers over her brood when a storm breaks or when an enemy approaches. But the rabbis, the scribes, and other religious leaders in Jerusalem were unwilling to submit to Christ (v.37b). See also Isaiah 65:2.

The city had been warned to repent by various prophets, including Jesus Himself. The apostles would soon begin to preach "repentance and the remission of sins in His name among all nations, beginning at Jerusalem" (Luke 24:47). But the obstacle to salvation was that these rebellious Jews "would not." As a result, they brought upon themselves the fearful calamities of AD 70, after having ignored all avenues of escape.

And so, Jesus concludes in verse 38, "Your house is left unto you desolate" (see also Luke 13:35). In Matthew 24:15, Jesus referred to Daniel's "abomination of *desolation*" and applied that event to the time prior to the destruction of the nation. More than just the magnificent temple, God had relinquished claim to the rest of Jerusalem and to the entire nation as well. Covenant curses would come upon them because of disobedience. But the disciples of Christ would not be left desolate (John 14:18). Daniel long ago prophesied that "desolations are determined [for] upon the wing of abominations shall come one that maketh desolate" (9:27).

The Roman invaders would come to unleash devastation upon a godless nation. The destruction could have been avoided if the people had continued to abide in God's covenant with them. Instead, they refused to accept the responsibility of murdering God-sent prophets and of various transgressions against God's will, especially in their trust in self and in other earthly powers. God had to scatter the covenant breakers and destroy the temple and genealogical records which made possible qualification of descendants of Aaron to serve as high priests. Animal sacrifices by these very priests to demonstrate loyalty to God could no longer apply.

Finally, in verse 39, Matthew explained that God would be seen through the preaching of the gospel. Jesus said, "For I say unto you, ye shall not see me henceforth, till ye shall say, 'Blessed is he that cometh in the name of the Lord.' " The leaders of institutional Judaism would reject the message and would soon crucify the Lord of glory. But Christ would come in splendor within a generation to avenge the wrongs perpetrated by the once glorious nation.

EVENING ON A HOUSETOP – WOODCUT, CIRCA 1880 *(SEE PAGE 95)*

Structure of the Olivet Discourse

The substance of teaching as presented in the three synoptic reports of the discourse is summarized as follows:

Matthew 24	Mark 13	Luke 21
Four things before the End, 24:4-14	*Four things before the End, 13:5-13.*	*Three things before the End, 21:8-19.*
1. False Christs, great apostasy, 4, 5.	1. False Christs and a great apostasy, 5, 6.	1. False Christs, 8.
2. Wars, famines, earthquakes, 6-8.	2. Wars, earthquakes, famines, 7, 8.	2. Wars, earthquakes, famine, other signs, 9-11.
3. Persecution, betrayals, hatred, false prophets, 9-13.	3. Persecution, betrayals, hatred, putting to death, 9, 11-13.	3. Persecution, betrayals, putting to death, hatred, 12-19.
4. Gospel to all the world, 14.	4. Gospel to all the nations, 10.	
Three signs when the End is close at hand, 15-28.	*Three signs when the End is close at hand, 14-23.*	*Two signs when the End is close at hand, 20-24.*
1. The abomination of desolation, 15-18.	1. The abomination of desolation, 14-17.	1. Jerusalem compassed with armies, 20, 21.
2. The great tribulation, 19-22.	2. The great tribulation, 18-20.	2. The great tribulation, 22-24.
3. False Christs and prophets, 23-28.	3. False Christs, 21-23.	
Apocalyptic picture of the End and the Parousia, 29-31.	*Apocalyptic picture of the End and the Parousia, 24-27.*	*Apocalyptic picture of the End and the Parousia, 25-28.*
1. Sun and moon darkened, stars fall, powers of heaven shaken, 29.	1. Sun and moon darkened, stars fall, powers of heaven shaken, 24, 25.	1. Signs in sun, moon, stars; distress; powers of heaven shaken, 25, 26.
2. Sign of Son of man, coming in clouds with power and glory, 30.	2. Son of man in clouds with power and glory, 26.	2. Son of man in clouds with power and glory, 27.
3. Angel ministries, trumpet, gathering of the elect, 31.	3. Angel ministries, gathering of the elect, 27.	3. Redemption at hand, 28.
Counsels and warnings, 32-51.	*Counsels and warnings, 28-37.*	*Counsels and warnings, 29-36.*
1. Similitude of the fig tree, 32, 33.	1. Similitude of the fig tree, 28, 29.	1. Similitude of the fig tree, 29-31.
2. All to occur in THIS GENERATION, 34, 35.	2. All to occur in THIS GENERATION, 30, 31.	2. All to occur in THIS GENERATION, 32, 33.
3. Day and hour unknown, 36.	3. Day and hour unknown, 32.	
4. Admonition to watch, 42-51.	4. Admonition to watch, 33-37.	3. Admonition to watch, 34-36.

Chapter Six

INTRODUCTION TO THE
OLIVET DISCOURSE

A FTER LAMENTING over Jerusalem and declaring that His generation of unfaithful Jews would shoulder the blame for all the righteous blood shed from Abel to Zechariah (Matt. 23:34-36), Jesus departed from the temple, never to enter it again, into the outer area of the temple esplanade. His disciples remarked about the buildings and the massive walls and fortifications surrounding the outer court (Matt. 24:2). Particularly, the size and shape of the limestone blocks and the Herodian masonry works and the rich temple ornaments excited the disciples from the country province of Galilee (Mark 13:1).

At that time the temple was being beautified and reconstructed in great splendor by ambitious and arrogant King Herod, and it would not be fully completed until more than thirty years after Jesus' crucifixion. Josephus mentions that the hard, white ornate stones at the base were approximately 40 by 12 by 18 feet in length, width and height – dimensions larger than the conclusion of modern archaeologists, yet unusually gigantic stones, indeed. Here was architectural and artistic splendor as perhaps never had been seen anywhere.

Jerusalem was a city of royal palaces, imposing walls, gates and fine houses. Apart from other structures and isolated in grandeur stood the impressive 19-acre temple mount with its several courts, porches and balconies rising in a series of terraces. It had splendid colonnades, and gold and silver covered gates, posts and lintels. Topping it all was the gleaming marble-cloistered, cedar roof of the temple.

The two-chambered sanctuary looked like a mountain covered with snow, for any roof not covered with dazzling white marble was stoutly plated with gold. From afar, the roof reflected such a fierce blaze that, in Josephus' words, "those who endeavored to look at it were forced to turn away as if they had looked straight at the sun." Indeed, the magnificent buildings evoked the glorious admiration of both Jews and Gentiles of that day as a perfect specimen of craftsmanship. For art and beauty, they were collectively a true ancient wonder which surely would endure for generations upon end.

Jews throughout the empire knew of no city that compared with their beloved Jerusalem. Herod's temple was revered as the place of worship by all faithful believers of Yahweh. Of this imposing building, Jesus in response to the disciples' admiration of it, emphatically and stunningly prophesied that "there shall not be left one stone upon another that shall not be thrown down" (Matt. 24:2b).

Passing out of the city and through the valley of Jehoshapat, Jesus climbed the slope of the Mount of Olives with his disciples and sat down on its crest that overlooked the city and the sunbathed temple. Of all the permanent and secure things on earth, the wealthy temple with its massive stones in its substructure was regarded as indestructible.

Still startled and struck dumb by His brief announcement, as if thinking that a systematic stone by stone demolition of the temple was surely a rash prediction, four of the disciples, all Galilean fishermen, asked privately, "Tell us, when shall these things be? And what shall be the sign of thy coming and of the end of the world?" (Matt. 24:3). In Mark this verse reads, "What shall be the sign when these things are all about to be accomplished?" (13:4). Luke's parallel account says, "Teacher, when therefore shall these things be? And what shall be the sign when these things are about to come to pass?" (21:7).

The disciples' question about the destruction of the temple, and Jesus' lengthy answer in Matthew 24, Mark 13, and Luke 21, have been the source of many sensational pulpit sermons. Religious speculators make wide use of Jesus' "signs of impending destruction" – the wars, the earthquakes, famine, the arrival of false teachers, the preaching of the gospel to all the world, "the abomination of desolation," and the great tribulation – and assign them all to the time preceding a yet future "second coming" of Christ.

For the last two hundred years and more, millennialists have applied these "signs of the times" to contemporary events (for a few of these are present in *any* age) and declared that the end of the world and the Lord's return were imminent. Even today, evangelicals misuse the concepts discussed in Matthew 24 by declaring that the Lord is to return in *our* time.

By carefully comparing all three accounts of the disciples' question which led to Jesus' Olivet discourse, it is evident that the premillennial "second coming" could not have been the topic of His speech. There is no reference to a yet-future end of time or the final judgment. The disciples simply asked about the time when the temple would be destroyed. "Will there be any warnings? Give us the signs!" But the millennialists have taken it for granted that the disciples inquired about end of the world events, a misunderstanding partly brought about by the King James Version which incorrectly renders *æon* (age) as "world."

Can this assumption be correct, when at that moment in time the disciples did not believe that He would ever be killed, much less return at the time of the general last day resurrection? A few days before the occasion, when the disciples asked

Him about the destruction of the temple, Jesus told them that He would be killed during this visit to Jerusalem and would rise again, but Luke reports in parallel statements that His followers "understood none of these things; and this saying was hid from them, and they perceived not the things that were said" (Luke 18:31-34). The disciples harbored the idea that the Messiah would never experience death. Like many others, these men saw the prophecies as material, rather than spiritual.

In fact, this notion was so firmly rooted in their minds that when Jesus died on the cross their expectations immediately sank. "But we hoped that it was He who would redeem Israel," remarked one (Luke 24:21; see also Acts 1:6). Some had purchased spices for a proper burial. Others doubted that Jesus had actually risen, when approached with the news. Only after He had been seen did many understand that He would continue to abide. With no expectation of His dying and rising on the third day, how could the disciples possibly have been asking about His "second coming" – his final return?

What is meant, then, when the disciples asked, "What shall be the sign of thy coming and of the end of the world?" (Matt. 24:3). The Greek word "coming" is *parousia* or presence; the "end of the world" is, literally, "the consummation of the age." The coming is a divine one in power and spirit, in the destruction of the temple, which implies the devastation of the city as well, just as the destruction of the temple in 586 B.C. occurred at the time when all of Jerusalem was leveled.

The "consummation of the age" to Jesus' audience thus meant the termination of Jewish political and religious rule – *their* age – not a time thousands of years in the future. A paraphrase of the verse reads, "When will this existing state of things, this system be completed, wound up, brought to a conclusion?" Though the disciples appear to be asking two or three questions in Matthew (as many commentators contend), they are really asking but one. The structure of the sentence is Semitic parallelism where, by altering the term, the second and third questions expand and explain the first one.

Therefore, the questions in Matthew 24:3, Mark 13:4, and Luke 21:7, are all the same. There is no justification, either linguistically or historically, to divide Jesus' question into three parts, since the disciples were thinking only about the time when "one stone would not be left upon another" would come to pass. The event would come during their generation (Matt. 24:34), not in the far-flung future. On several previous occasions, He had told the disciples of the loss of life that would soon befall the Jews (Luke 13, 19, etc.). In the parable of the vineyard (Matt. 21:33-46), Jesus taught that God would destroy the Jewish nation. Its leaders realized that the parable was aimed at them (v. 45). Very likely Jesus related that story on the same day that He foretold the dismantling of the temple. The application, therefore, would be fresh on the minds of His followers.

At times the Jewish prophets taught that God would consign the temple to destruction under some circumstances. Before it happened, Jeremiah said that the Jerusalem of his day would be in flames instigated by Nebuchadnezzar's army (21:10; 37:8-10). Ezekiel recorded the movement of the glory of the Lord through the temple and out of it (8:1-6, 10:19). At that time God was executing divine judgment in wrath, the likely understanding of Christ's disciples .

Jesus' followers therefore did not associate the "coming" and "end of the world – *aeon*" of Matthew 24:3 with the final return of Christ together with the destruction of this planet. Instead, this word and phrase are different ways of expressing the time when Jerusalem would be conquered militarily and finally destroyed. Jesus also used the phrase "end of the age" in the Parable of the Tares (Matt. 13:39-40), as occurring when angels would separate the wicked from the just (v. 49), denoting His presence with the disciples always "even unto the consummation of the age" (Matt. 28:20).

Therefore, the "coming" and "end of the age" refers to the era of which they were a part and had knowledge. This age is the seventieth week of Daniel 9:24-27; a total of 69 of these weeks had passed by the time the Messiah was "cut off" at Calvary. The "abomination of desolation" in Daniel's seventieth week is fulfilled at Matthew 24:15, according to what Jesus Himself said.

Thus, any idea that these "signs of the times" portend the end of time and a future final judgment of the world rests upon a misinterpretation of Matthew 24:3 and the rest of the chapter. The utter destruction – "There shall not be left here one stone upon another" – was emphatically fulfilled in the year 70 when Titus' Roman army marched upon Judea and razed the glorious temple after successfully conquering Jerusalem.

Just as the prophet Haggai described the building of the temple as "a stone being laid upon a stone" (2:15), Jesus now expressed its destruction by the proverbial statement "one stone not being left upon another." Such a phrase hyperbolically denotes very exemplary destruction, not literal fulfillment, allowing the possibility of some foundation stones and parts of walls to remain in place.

The Word "Coming" in Matthew 24-25

Two Greek words, *parousia* and *erchomai,* are translated "coming" in Jesus' Olivet discourse. Both words carry the general meaning of a presence or a coming and going. The final return of Christ which is yet future, the coming of Jesus in the destruction of Jerusalem, and individually to each of the seven city ekklesia of Asia (Rev. 2-3), and the ordinary comings and goings of mortal men, all may be expressed by either Greek word. Context is paramount in determining the application of *parousia* and *erchomai* in Matthew 24-25; it cannot be determined by the meaning of the word itself.

Both of these Greek words appear often in Matthew's construction of Jesus' sermon, from 24:1 to 25:46. *Parousia,* coming or presence, is part of the phrase "coming of the Son of man" in 24:27, 37, 39. In 24:3, *parousia* is included in the phrase "sign of thy coming." The Greek verb *erchomai* is translated "coming" in phrases which tell of the "son of man coming [or cometh]" or "the Lord cometh" as in 24:30, 40, 44, 46, 48; 25:31. (The word come, *heko*, is associated with the slavemaster in 24:50.)

Parousia denotes "both an arrival, and a consequent presence with" (W. E. Vine, *Expository Dictionary of New Testament Words,* p. 210). The word means presence, as opposed to absence, as in Philippians 2:12, where Paul speaks of his readers' obedience not only when he was with them but also when he was away. *Parousia* is also properly rendered coming, especially regarding the appearance of Christ in His kingdom (compare Matt. 16:27-28 and 24:30, 25:31; Rev. 1:7-9 and 22:7; see also John 14:3). It is the technical term in Koine Greek for the visit of an emperor or other ruler (G. Abbot-Smith, *Lexicon,* p. 347). See also the *Testament of Judah 22:2.*

Gerhard Kittel concludes that "the *parousia* concept is one of the original stones in the synoptic tradition concerning Jesus" (*Theological Dictionary of the New Testament, V*:866-867). "It is present in fully developed form in the *parousia* address in Mark 13 [Matt. 24], which, strongly influenced though it is by Jewish and primitive Christian apocalyptic, has crystallized around genuine dominical sayings. . . " F. Wilbur Gingrich (as well as Thayer) sees *parousia* as a coming, an arrival of human beings (as in II Cor. 7:6f, Phil 1:26) or of Christ and His messianic advent at the end of the age (as expressed in Matthew 24).

Concerning the questions asked in Matthew 24:3, *The Pulpit Commentary* sees all events thus asked about as synchronous, or very closely connected. A. T. Robertson says that there is no way to answer if these events were to take place simultaneously, [yet] seeing the destruction of Jerusalem in AD 70 as a symbol of a yet future second coming (*Word Pictures of the New Testament, I:* 187-188).

Erchomai essentially means the same as *parousia,* denoting the action of the coming (presence). *Erchomai* appears in Matthew 16:28, "the Son of man coming in His kingdom" and in Mark 9:1 "the kingdom of God coming in power." See also Luke 17:20-21, John 10:10, 11:27 and several instances between John 14:1 - 16:13 and in Revelation 2-3. John stresses the necessity of belief that Jesus is *erchomai* in the flesh (I John 4:2,3; 5:20; II John 7), a truth which coincides with the "doctrine of Christ" of II John 9.

The references above emphasize that Christ would come again, doing so on the Pentecost of Acts 2, in the destruction of Jerusalem in AD 70, and in appearances to Paul and others (Acts 9:17, I Cor. 15:1f). He will return at the end of time to claim his own, as He delivers the kingdom to the Father (I Cor. 15:24) and judges the wicked. Evidently, the "coming" of Christ does not refer to *just one* historical event. There were a number of these days of judgment, *parousia,* as also implied in Jesus' phrase "one of the days of the Son of man" (Luke 17:22).

The chapters which follow show that *parousia / erchomai* in Matthew 24:1-25:30 exclusively refers to Jesus as ruler of the kings of the earth coming in judgment in AD 70 to execute vengeance against the city of Jerusalem and destroy its temple. The associative language – Jesus coming on clouds, the darkening of the heavens, the collapse of elements, the flight of eagles from afar – all are familiar forms of apocalyptic themes appropriated from the Hebrew prophets to mark the termination of the Jewish age with the conquest of Jerusalem. Jesus emphasized that some of the generation of His audience (24:34) would survive to see the fulfillment of *all* things about which the disciples inquired in Matthew 24:3. The discerning man of God would see the influence of Christ in it all, i.e., His *parousia* or presence.

Chapter Seven

THE SIGNS OF CHRIST'S COMING

A FTER ANNOUNCING the destruction of the temple within the generation of His disciples (Matt. 24:34), Jesus foretold many signs of impending destruction which would mark the end or completion of the age. They are related in verses 4 to 15 of Matthew 24.

The Advent of False Christs

Jesus began His Olivet discourse by announcing the arrival of religious pretenders prior to the end: "For many shall come in my name, saying, I am the Christ; and shall lead many astray." (v. 5). History does not record the names of false christs before the siege of Titus upon Jerusalem, insist premillennial commentators. But since the unscrupulous would not leave enduring institutions behind, they escaped the specific notice of contemporary writers.

The Jewish historian Josephus, an eyewitness to most of the things he relates, recorded in his famous histories that "the land was overrun with magicians, robbers, seducers, and imposters, who drew the people after them into solitudes and deserts to see the signs and miracles which they promised to show them by the power of God." Since Josephus avoided mention of the people of Christ, he never calls any of these various pretenders "false christs" but rather "false prophets."

To Matthew's words about false christs, Luke adds, "The time draweth near" (21:8b). Indeed, soon after the apostles began to preach (as recorded in Acts) Simon Magus appeared, bewitching the saints in Samaria (Acts 8:9-10). Of similar character was Dositheus the Samaritan, a Christ-pretender and a wonder worker, according to Origen. During the latter days of Nero's reign, which ended in the year 68, Josephus said that impostors emerged so frequently that they were apprehended and killed every day, undoubtedly an exaggeration.

In about AD 44, an impostor named Theudas persuaded about 400 people to bring their possessions to the River Jordan, where he promised to divide the river for their safe passage out of Judea (see Acts 5:36). But when the procurator of Judea heard about these things, he sent a troop of horsemen upon the party and surprised them, killing many and scattering others. Theudas himself was captured and decapitated, and his head was displayed in Jerusalem, as recorded by both Josephus and Eusebius (*Hist. Eccl.* 2.11.1-3).

On another occasion, when the Romans occupied Jerusalem in the late 60s, an Egyptian Jewish false prophet led 4000 people into the Judean wilderness (Acts 21:38), promising them that he would make the city walls fall flat as did those of Jericho centuries earlier. According to Eusebius, thousands of Jews assembled on the Mount of Olives, and prepared to swarm into Jerusalem and rescue the city from the Romans. But the Roman legions anticipated the attack and subdued the throng, taking captive or killing most of the Egyptian's followers (*Hist. Eccl.* 2.21.1-3).

"Wars and Rumors of Wars . . ."

The reassuring expression in verse 6, "and ye shall hear of wars and rumors of wars; see that ye be not troubled: for these things must needs come to pass . . ." has been applied by people throughout the centuries to their day and time. Actually, they pointed to the years of instability just before 70, not only in Judea but throughout the Roman Empire. During that time, Gentile uprisings occurred against the Jews, as well as threats of Roman attack upon Judea.

Fighting erupted in the city, after various factions formed their own armies. Jewish revolutionaries took advantage of the general disturbances to gain riches for themselves at the expense of kinsmen. Four ancient historians, including Josephus, told of various skirmishes in such places as Jerusalem before AD 50, in Mesopotamia, Caeserea, Scythopolis, Alexandria, Ashkelon, and Damascus. In all, thousands of Jews were either killed or imprisoned.

After Emperor Nero's violent death in Rome in June of 68, disorder reigned everywhere. The empire rocked as minor revolts flared in various provinces. Six months later Nero's successor, Galba, was overthrown by Otho, who in turn died violently three months later and was replaced by Vitellius. He, too, was knifed in a fresh wave of infighting, and Vespasian assumed the throne. Within a year three Roman emperors fell to the sword.

"For nation shall rise against nation, and kingdom against kingdom . . . " (v. 7) echoes Isaiah, who, during a similar time of great unrest in Egypt in about 720 B.C., stated, "City shall fight against city and kingdom against kingdom (19:2; compare II Chron. 15:6). Such language conveys a vivid impression of national tumult and civil strife, and Jesus appropriately used the same language to refer to the seditions, insurrections, revolts, and local wars, which preceded the destruction of Jerusalem. The "rumors of wars" (v. 6) refer to the conflicting and exaggerated reports which preceded the approach of armies and led to panic. Anxiety of war is a common Old Testament theme (Isa. 13:4-5, 19:1a; Jer. 4:19-22; Joel 2:4-9, 3:9-11; Nah. 2:3-5, etc.).

Amid all of the trouble, the disciples had to maintain calm, reasonable minds, and not be unsettled by the disturbances. Remarkably, the predictions by Jesus were made during a time when the Roman world basked in peace and the Jewish nation enjoyed full imperial protection.

Famine and Pestilence

As a result of wars there were often shortages of food, spreading famine, pestilence, and desolation. In verse 7b Jesus foretells of "famines and earthquakes in diverse places." Four famines raged during the reign of Claudius (one of them is mentioned in Acts 11:28); others occurred in Italy, Judea, and Greece in subsequent years. More than 30,000 died of pestilence in ancient Babylon and in parts of Judea and in Rome before aD 70, as recorded by Josephus and Eusebius. Food was scarce in Palestine during all of AD 68-70. During one extended Judean famine, the Jewish queen Helen spent large sums purchasing grain in Egypt for distribution to the needy (Eusebius, *Hist. Eccl.* 2.12.1-3).

Earthquakes and Great Signs

Jesus also promised that earthquakes would occur in various places (v. 7b). Earthquakes indeed have had their place in descriptions of God's intervention in history (Judg. 5:5; Psa. 18:13-14, 68:8, 77:18, 114:7; Isa. 24:19, 29:6, 64:1), demonstrating God's power and divine judgment (Job 9:6, Isa. 13:13, Amos 9:1, Ezek. 38:19-20, Zech. 14:5). During Nero's reign, aD 54-68, Pompeii was virtually destroyed, and Rome also suffered damage; in AD 61 an earthquake demolished Laodicea and other localities in Asia Minor. Other "diverse places" included Crete, Smyrna, Miletus, Chios, Samos, and Campania, each of which experienced a mid-first century earthquake.

Earthquakes thus symbolically preceded the end of the Jewish age (Mark 13:8. Luke 21:11), demonstrating God's power over earthly events. In a Dead Sea Scrolls document, God controls political events as well, as in the statement, "The mountains quake before Him, and the hills heave and the earth [is lifted up] before Him" *(Commentary on Nahum.* See also *II Baruch* 27:7).

At this point Luke adds to the discourse, "There shall be fearful sights and great signs from heaven . . . " Josephus recorded various omens and prodigies which preceded the fall of Jerusalem. He related that a "star hung over the city like a sword, and a comet continued for a whole year." Late in the decade of 60, when the Jews gathered to celebrate the feast of the unleavened bread, a green light allegedly shone above the temple's altar for about a half hour, as bright as if it were sunlight. At about that same time an animal led by a priest to sacrifice brought forth a lamb in the midst of the temple.

Josephus also recited a story about the temple's brass east gate, so heavy that it usually took 20 men to shut and fasten by strong bars and bolts. One night it opened spontaneously and could not be shut again. In connection, chariots and armies were seen fighting in the clouds and besieging cities. All of these signs smack strongly of being mere apocryphal stories, though the Roman historian Tacitus also mentions some of them.

Beginning in about AD 63, a certain countryman initiated a strange ritual which he carried out especially during the time of the great festivals. He would run up and down the streets of the holy city day and night, shouting, "A voice from the east, a voice from the west! A voice from the four winds, a voice against Jerusalem and the temple! A voice against the bridegroom and the brides, a voice against all people."

Various magistrates tried to restrain him by beatings and torture, but he continued to cry mournfully, "Woe, woe, to Jerusalem!" The man uttered his outcries for nearly seven years, growing neither hoarse nor tired. He had begun this practice when the city was at peace and still had riches, continuing until finally one day a stone from a sling struck him dead. Perhaps these stories emanated from disordered imaginations, yet among the citizens of Jerusalem they had the effect of prophetic realities.

Persecution and Trials

Verse 8, "But all these things are merely the beginning of travail," is a recurring Old Testament image of divine judgment (Isa. 13:8, 26:17, 66:7-9; Mic. 4:9-10; Hos. 13:13; Jer. 4:31, 6:24, 13:21, 22:23, 49:22, 50:43). A time of great trouble and calamity upon a certain people is often expressed metaphorically by the pains of a woman in labor. This phrasing also alludes to the Jewish idea of the birth pangs of the Messiah. In his *Annals,* the Roman Tacitus described this period of intense suffering, AD 66-70, as one "rich in calamities, horrible with battles, rent with seditions." These things occurred at the beginning of birth pangs, portending even more fearful troubles. But God's people could face turbulence with confidence and the assurance that they would be delivered.

In Verse 9, Jesus foretold the death of saints at the hands of fanatical Jews, and later Nero's soldiers: "Then shall they deliver you up unto tribulation, and shall kill you: and you shall be hated of all the nations for my name's sake." Jesus Himself said that His followers would be scourged in the synagogue (Matt. 10:17, Mark 13:9, Luke 12:11). In the decade of 60, the Jewish Zealots set up sham courts in Jerusalem and dragged kinsmen before them.

More definitely, the book of Acts shows fulfillment of verse 9. Peter and John were imprisoned (4:1-3); Stephen was stoned (7:59); Herod laid violent hands on Christians and killed John's brother, James (12:1-2); Paul and his companions were beaten (16:23), stoned (14:19), brought before the judgment seats (18:12), and threatened with scourging and imprisonment (22:23-24). According to strong tradition, Paul was killed in Rome and Peter was crucified (John 21:18-19) before AD 70 (see *I Clement* 5). As the church father Tertullian put it, it was a war against the very name of Christ.

Nero's persecution in Rome during AD 64-65 involved exquisite torture of the hated Christians. Tacitus wrote, "Mockery of every sort was added to their deaths. Covered with the skins of wild beasts, they were torn by mad dogs and perished, or were even nailed to crosses, or were doomed to the flames and burnt, to serve as nightly illumination, when daylight had expired." Historian Philip Schaff adds, "Christian men and women covered with pitch or oil or resin, and nailed to posts of pine, were lighted and burned as torches for the amusement of the mob; while Nero, in fantastical dress, figured in a horse race, and displayed his art as a charioteer" (*History of the Christian Church, Vol. I*, pp. 381-382).

Though delivered to local Jewish councils, the saints would not be abandoned in tribunal situations. The faithful were not to worry, since the Holy Spirit would provide knowledge and unanswerable responses—"a mouth and a wisdom" (Luke 21:15, comp. 12:11-12). Thus, without premeditation, they could speak boldly as apologists before governors and kings (Mark. 13:9-11). The gospel mission would result in painful family divisions and betrayal (v. 12). Among the Jewish people there had never been a time of more desperate religious zeal and fanaticism than the decade preceding the fall of the city and temple.

Apostasy

In verses 11-12, Jesus told of the rise of false prophets who would lead many astray. Paul warns of deceitful men masquerading as workers of Christ (II Cor. 11:13-15). In Galatia, some had distorted the gospel (1:7), while others would abandon their Lord. The books of II Peter and Jude also told of many who followed false teachers who subtly introduced heresies. The letter to the Hebrews warned against apostasy and unbelief (3:7-8, 6:4-8, 10:26-39), graphically describing the perils of falling away (See 6:4, 10:38).

Thus, during AD 66-70, many departed from the faith rather than suffer for the Christ. False prophets did arise. Iniquity multiplied, eating the heart out of authentic spiritual faith. Jesus promised salvation for the faithful, not only in the afterlife, but also from the physical distress of the tribulation prior to the destruction of Jerusalem.

Jesus also said that many "shall deliver up one another and shall hate one another" (v. 10). Traitors yielding to ungodly pressures to disclose information to authorities would betray kinsmen, and a man's most dreadful foes may well have been family members (Mark 13:12). Tacitus reported that several Jews were seized who confessed the presence of others, and thus a great many citizens were convicted and barbarously executed.

Because of false teachers arising from within, and external tribulation, the love of many saints would "wax cold." The lukewarm would desert, corrupt or become indifferent to the faith. But all who withstood seductions arising from every hand, "enduring to the end" would be saved—that is, their lives would be spared during the tribulation upon Jerusalem prior to AD 70, and also, because of abiding, overcoming faith, they would maintain the salvation of their souls.

Truly, the Lord is able to deliver the godly from temptations (II Peter 2:9), for Jesus Himself promised that not a hair on the head of the faithful would perish during the time of Jerusalem's distress (Luke 21:18). Here is a great example of God's providence, for Christians late in the decade of 60 heeded the warnings of Matthew 24 and escaped from Jerusalem before the city was sealed off by the Romans. Tradition discloses that messianic Jews fled eastward across the Jordan River to relocate in Pella, staying there until after the holy city fell in AD 70 (Eusebius, *Hist. Eccl.* 3.5.3).

Verse 14 declares that the gospel had to be preached to all of the world before the end should come—"the consummation of the age" (see v. 3). Premillennialists apply this event to a future end of the world and insist that only after certain Third World nations and tribes are evangelized, Jesus will reappear. But this application mishandles Paul's plain words to the Colossians, in which he declared that ". . . the gospel which ye heard. . . . was preached in all creation under heaven" (1:23; see also 1:5-6). The early saints journeyed everywhere, preaching the word (Acts 8:4, 11:19; Mark 16:20).

The book of Acts chronicles only a small part of the gospel efforts by a fraction of the apostles and evangelists. But even their writings show that the gospel was disseminated widely within a generation, taking root throughout the Roman Empire. By AD 64, when Nero set fire to his own city, Rome, Christians had become a potent force, able to arouse the jealousy of the government. Late in the first century, Clement of Rome said that, toward the end of Nero's reign, Paul "taught righteousness to the whole world . . . both in the east and west" (*I Clement* 5).

In connection with the apostle, the same writer rhetorically asked about the united labors of the rest of the apostles, knowing that they labored mightily. An early tradition insists that the apostles had preached the gospel to all the world, even beyond the sea to the "Britannic Isles." The Bible itself discloses that evangelists scattered in a worldwide penetration of the gospel (Rom. 1:8; 10:15, 18; 16:25-26). "All the world" embraces that part ruled by Rome (see Luke 2:1).

The Abomination of Desolation

Verse 15 portentously introduces the abomination of deso-lation: "When therefore ye see the abomination of desolation, which was spoken of through Daniel the prophet, standing in the holy place. . ." It is, literally, "the appalling horror," a con-cept which was spoken through Daniel as a undefined person standing in the holy place (see 9:27, 12:11). Mark's account reads essentially the same as Matthew's, qualitatively defining the "holy place" by adding "standing where he ought not" (13:14). This abomination would be a distinctive sign to the Judean disciples to ready themselves for departure from the city (vv. 16-20).

Unfortunately, the nature of the abomination is imprecise. Many commentators refer it to the actions of heathen con-querors during and after the siege of the Jerusalem temple. According to that view, the planting of the Roman army's standards outside of the city would be an abomination, because it was pagan, and a desolation, because the Romans conquered by devastating their enemies. Some see the abomination as the internal desecration of the temple by the Jewish Zealots, under the pretense of defending it.

Other interpretations are offered, including the millennial reference to the time before the "second coming," though the destruction of Jerusalem satisfies them as a partial fulfillment. Such a rendering ignores both the historical and literary con-text of Jesus' plain words. In interpreting this difficult passage, it must be determined what is specifically identified, and rea-son from the known to the unknown.

The language of Matthew 24:15 unmistakably emanates from the writings of the Jewish prophets and scribes. When the "abomination that maketh desolate" appeared nearly 200 years previously, God abandoned His protective care of the temple (Dan. 11:31-32). In about 165 B.C. the Syrian ruler Antiochus Epiphanes advanced upon Jerusalem, entering the city on the Sabbath and butchering the unresisting inhabitants. The Syrian soldiers pillaged at will and carried off women and children for sale as slaves. City walls and houses were razed while Antiochus seized possession of the temple.

The Syrians offered swine's flesh on a temple altar, and prevented faithful Jews from celebrating the Sabbath. *I Maccabees* 1:54-63 records how Antiochus entered the sanctuary and removed the golden altar, the candlestick of light, and the temple vessels (1:21). The Syrians also erected a small altar dedicated to the Greek god Zeus (see *I Macc.* 1:54), worshipping in a sacred place.

As in the time of Antiochus, the desolation of verse 15 also meant that the temple would be emptied of worshippers. On the pain of death this leader effectually suspended the Jewish religion, burning copies of the scriptures containing the law and turning the rooms of priests and temple chambers into places where men dallied with harlots. The abandonment of temple gatherings was prompted by an abomination so detestable that God's saints forsook the temple, thus provoking the desolation.

The mid-first century abomination also has religious character, since it is connected with the holy place. It is a profaning of the temple sanctuary in some way (see Dan. 9:27, 11:32a), implying sacrilegious acts. To perform a sacrilege, a degree of religious commitment is necessary and thus the source of the corruption came from its internal spiritual makeup, the nation's religious light. It involved a perversion of the covenant and a taking away of the continual burnt offerings (Dan. 11:31). Therefore, any Roman heathen sacrifices and idolatrous acts by its soldiers are ruled out.

The abomination of Matthew 24:15 would be unmistakable and easy for messianic Jews to recognize late in the decade of 60. Upon seeing it, believers were to flee from Jerusalem (v. 16). If confined to the temple it would be apparent to all within the city; there is no hint that the abomination is a revived Antiochus or some other foreigner.

Mark's parallel account (13:14, A.S.V.) provides a vital clue to an understanding of the passage. "But when you see the abomination of desolation standing where he ought not to be . . . " This rendering recognizes the neuter language of "abomination of desolation" and the masculine use of the word "standing." The *New English Bible* has it, "When you see the abomination of desolation, usurping a place which is not *his* . . . ."

Therefore a male sacrilege was involved. It came from within the nation. Fulfillment very likely occurred during the time the Zealots profaned the temple during the winter of 67 and 68. They held the temple under heavy arms, allowed the feet of criminals to crowd into the hallowed places, and perpetrated murders in the temple itself.

The precise abomination that emptied the temple—an event that signaled the time for God's people to flee from Jerusalem—probably came when the Zealots themselves, together with robbers and other ignoble persons, cast lots and installed as high priest an imbecile, the unrighteous Phanni, who thus "usurped a position that was not his." He was entirely ignorant of priestly duties, but as a "man of the people" his wickedness coincided with the Zealots' deeds. On that occasion, Ananus, the utterly shocked outgoing high priest, left in tears and bemoaned the future of the Jewish priesthood. He reportedly said, "I would rather have died first, before I had seen the house of God so full of abominations."

At that very time, other priests were killed and drunkenness and all sorts of wickedness took place inside the temple. Soon the God-ordained daily sacrifices were suspended. Nothing remained unpolluted, and the enemies of the temple aristocracy contemptuously trod under foot the whole glory of God, as well as the law itself.

The Zealots' seditious acts also included the admitting of the bloodthirsty Idumaean warriors into the temple area. Early in the year 68 a bloodbath occurred and 8500 people were said to have perished in battle. Any member of priestly caste

was hunted down and slain. Josephus wrote that the vil-
lainous Zealots "trampled upon all the laws of men and
laughed at the laws of God. . . . They ridiculed [the
prophets] as the tricks of jugglers."

Thus native hands first polluted the sacred precincts before
God abandoned the temple as the locus of His glory. Faithful
disciples left after Phanni's investiture. Luke's parallel account
considers the arrival of military forces in the area during the
winter of AD 68 as the second signal for flight: "But when you
see Jerusalem compassed by *armies*, then know that her desolation is at hand" (Luke 21:20). Fulfillment likely came in AD
66 during the first Roman siege and also when the Idumaeans
were encamped for several weeks on and about Mount Olivet
and in other places near the city. Thus the desolation would
come soon thereafter (Luke 21:20b), for God would withdraw His protection. Therefore, the prophecy of the
abomination of desolation was fulfilled two years before the
Romans destroyed the temple late in the summer of 70.

The abomination of desolation is obviously not a yet future event to occur during a tribulation period in
connection with the rapture of the saints, together with a
temple restoration in Jerusalem. Instead, the abomination
points to a past fulfillment, having taken place when the
pagan Idumaeans were encamped around the holy place,
the city of Jerusalem, in the year 68.

Every second to fourth century church father who commented upon the abomination of desolation declared that it
had already taken place. In *Stromata* 1.21, Clement of Alexandria saw the abomination as occurring in Nero's day (see also
Irenaeus, *Against Heresies* 5.25.4-5). Hippolytus' *Treatise on
Christ and Antichrist*, 62-63, quoted Matthew 24:15-22 and
Daniel 12:11-12 and applied them to no specific events,
only past general tribulation and persecution. *The Commentary on the Apocalypse* by Victorinus mentions the
"contempt" (the abomination) as a turning away from salvation because of idolatry.

The fourth century Syrian, John Chrysostom, directly related the abomination of desolation to the decline of Jerusalem by the acts of Roman soldiers, while the apocryphal *Recognitions of Clement* associated the event with the destruction of the temple. The renowned St. Augustine also said that the abomination took place when Jerusalem was overthrown, quoting Luke 21:20 to sustain his point.

The parenthetical "let the reader understand" (Matt. 24:15b) was Jesus' plea for all to note the prophetic background of such concepts as the abomination of desolation (see Dan. 2:21-23, 9:25a, 12:10b; Rev. 1:3). Even for anyone today, an understanding of Matthew 24 is impossible without a knowledge of the Jewish prophets and recognizing the nature of Oriental symbolic language.

The Disciples Flee from Jerusalem

Verse 16, "then let them that are in Judea flee unto the mountains . . ." begins a section that describes a local first century Judean situation of impending Roman invasion. The time cannot be at the final return of Christ, when flight would be useless, for one could not avoid God's wrath by hiding in the mountains. Jesus addressed messianic Jews *only,* and not modern mixed races throughout the world who have never seen or have no knowledge of Jerusalem.

Flight to avoid judgment is still another Old Testament theme. In Genesis 19:17 Lot's wife fled into the mountains from abominable Sodom. See also Luke 17:28-29. It was an urgent flight, as in Ezekiel 7:15-16, wherein the fate of those who did not flee before the destruction of Jerusalem in 586 B.C. is vividly described: "The sword is without, and the pestilence and famine within: he that is in the field shall die with a sword; and he that is in the city, famine and pestilence shall devour him. But those of them that escape shall escape, and shall be on the mountain like doves of the valley, all of them moaning every one in his iniquity." See also Jeremiah 16:16 and Zechariah 14:5b.

Jerusalem's God-fearers had to flee to escape the terrible punishment that would come upon Judea because of the sacrilege in the temple (Matt. 24:15), and other Jewish transgressions, including those against Jesus and the early Christian saints. Refuge would be in the mountains, which Roman armies would generally avoid. David fled to caves to escape danger (I Sam. 22:1, Psa. 11:1). Others in past times similarly hid (Josh. 10:16, I Sam. 13:6).

Verses 17-18 tell of the urgency of the flight: no delay! Jesus said that anyone seeing an advance of enemy forces from the house top should not enter his house but rather speedily escape out of the city gates as fast as he possibly could. The flat-topped roofs of dwellings throughout Jerusalem were regularly walked upon (some had tables and chairs for casual social occasions); many had exterior stairs to allow an ascent or descent without entering the house itself. The dwellings thus formed continuous terraces from one end of Jerusalem to the other, terminating at city gates.

Thus, a man on a rooftop could run upon his neighbors' flat-roofed dwellings and out the city gates and escape from an approaching army. He must not waste time entering his dwelling to pack his possessions, for an attempt to carry them might impede flight. Similarly, Jesus stated that farmers and other fieldworkers on the adjacent hillsides and in the valleys should not return to their houses within the city for extra clothing.

Such hyperbolic expressions to emphasize the urgency to leave Jerusalem intimate that flight from the city might have to be as sudden and hasty as Lot's was out of Sodom. Therefore, watch! (Mark 13:37). After an announcement that the Romans were in full battle march in the Judean lowlands heading toward Jerusalem, faithful disciples could not afford the luxury of lingering in the area. The invaders would surround the city so rapidly and close it off that every precious hour was needed to escape.

Verses 19-20 state possible deterrents to a successful flight: "But woe unto them that are with child, and to them that give suck, in those days! And pray ye that your flight be not in the winter, neither on a Sabbath." Evidently, Jesus had compassion for pregnant and nursing mothers, for the wintertime and the Sabbath also would hinder a successful departure. The cold wet Judean winters also meant short days and bad roads. Seasonal heavy rains occasionally made desert streams impassable torrents, but God would answer earnest prayers to avoid hardships in travel.

A departure on the Sabbath would be virtually impossible, because Jerusalem's gates would be closed (Neh. 13:19-22), and the securing of even modest provisions would be difficult. The shortness of the Sabbath day's journey—about $7/_{10}$ of a modern mile—also might restrict movement. Otherwise, there might be persecution for breaking the law. If Christ were speaking of a future end time "second coming," none of these events would apply. But all of them fit nicely within the AD 66-70 time period.

Verses 21 and 22, which discuss the great tribulation, mention the reasons for the flight, while verses 23 and 24 warn of false Christs who would deter leaving Jerusalem. This "great tribulation" has been the touchstone of much speculation. Premillennialists insist that it will occur at the "second coming" of Christ which will be preceded by all of the signs of the discourse which begins at verse 3.

Premillennialism declares that, prior to His future final coming, titanic world wars would engulf nations (see v. 6), and famines would rage. Disease, epidemics and pestilence would ravage cities and countrysides, while great earthquakes would rend and convulse the land (v. 7). A final persecution would inflict His followers, and false ministers would arise (vv. 9-11), amid an age of lawlessness, of rampant iniquity, and a great breakdown of morality. The gospel would be carried to every nation, including those in the heart of Africa (v. 14). There would be unprecedented tribulation so great that nobody would be saved unless those days would be shortened by Christ's appearance (v. 22). In that statement, premillennialists insist that only since World War II has the world ever been threatened by the possibility of stark annihilation because of the stockpile of nuclear weapons, even a portion of which would be capable of wiping out all inhabitants of the earth.

The millennialists believe that this tribulation will occur at the time of the "rapture"—the occasion when God's saints are supposed to be caught up with Jesus into the air above the earth, citing I Thessalonians 4:16-17—while the earth itself experiences seven years of terrible distress. Interestingly, premillennial church fathers of the second and third centuries never held such views. As recorded by Matthew, Jesus plainly said that the disciples were to flee to the mountains when the tribulation begins! (see v. 16). Thus, saints would be on earth at the time of the so-called celestial rapture.

Women nursing babies (v. 19) especially would be subject to delay, and everyone would need divine assistance to avoid travel on the Sabbath or in the dead of winter. Assuredly, at the time of the great tribulation (v. 21), one's eternal destiny would not depend on such things! These facts taken together show the fallacy of the premillennial reign theory. Therefore, in verses 16-21, Jesus is indeed describing, almost forty years before their occurrence, the great Jewish Wars and the devastation of Judea during the years 66-70.

STREET SCENE, 19TH CENTURY JERUSALEM

Chapter Eight

THE GREAT TRIBULATION –
MATTHEW 24:21

T HROUGHOUT THE FIRST twenty verses of Matthew 24, Jesus related to His disciples the many events which would accompany His "coming" against Jerusalem in AD 70 at the time when the temple would be destroyed. Several signs are mentioned in detail; many of the expressions of Matthew 24, and its parallels Mark 13 and Luke 21, are also found in prophecies and apocalyptic passages in the Old Testament concerning the fall of ancient nations and cities.

Jesus declared that the "abomination of desolation" (v. 15), first prophesied by Daniel (see 9:27, 12:11), was one of the events which would take place at the time of the famines, earthquakes, wars, false prophets, etc. (vv. 3-11). These all found fulfillment in the years immediately before the destruction of Jerusalem. Before the Roman enemy would begin a lengthy siege, the disciples were warned to flee to the mountains (v. 16) in haste (vv. 17-18). They would pray that their flight would not be in the cold of wintertime or on the Sabbath, when travel would be restricted (vv. 19-20).

Despite Jesus' statements specifically directed to people who could apply the signs to mid first century events in Judea, modern millennial speculators ignore historical fact and apply everything in the future to the generation of His final coming, in prelude to the end time judgment. Verses 21-22 provide the fuel for that view: "For then shall be great tribulation, such as hath not been from the beginning of the world until now, no, nor ever shall be. And except those days had been shortened, no flesh would have been saved: but for the elect's sake those days shall be shortened."

Contrary to the premillennial assignment of these verses to the great tribulation preceding Christ's "second coming" is the phrase, ". . . from the beginning of the world until now, no, nor ever shall be." That phrase begs a comparison of the present with both past and future miseries. It most certainly contemplates a period after the event – that there would be additional sufferings, less in intensity for sure, but other sufferings, nevertheless. Verse 22 therefore cannot be applied to the premillennialist's end time tribulation, for that theory does not allow for any *future* tribulations. Any end time application removes the statement from its context.

This declaration of an unprecedented tribulation unequaled before or since exemplifies the hyperbolic language of judgment often used by Jewish prophets. When Jeremiah wrote, "Alas! For that day is great, so that none is like it: it is even the time of Jacob's trouble . . . " (30:7), he told of the deliverance of Israel from captivity through judgment upon the nations. Babylon was their yoke.

In another instance, Joel symbolically spoke of a day of judgment of Israel by ". . . a great people and a strong; there hath not been ever the like, neither shall there be any more after them, even to the years of many generations" (2:2). Of Jerusalem, Ezekiel said, "And I will do in thee that which I have not done, and whereunto I will not do any more the like, because of all thine abominations" (5:9), words strikingly similar to those used by Jesus more than 600 years later (see also Ex. 10:14, 11:6; Dan. 9:12, 12:1; I Kgs. 3:12; II Kgs, 18:5).

I Maccabees 9:27 uses this same proverbial expression by stating, "There was great affliction in Israel, the like whereof was not since the time that a prophet was not seen amongst them. . ." (see also the *Testament of Moses* 8:1). Of Jerusalem's tribulation before AD 70, Josephus wrote that "the multitude of those that perished exceeded all of the destructions which either man or God ever brought upon the world. . . . No other city ever suffered such things, no other generation was ever more fruitful in wickedness." Matthew 24:21 thus conforms to the ancient pattern of writing, which describes as unprecedented catastrophe a judgment of a select people.

Matthew couches this tribulation – the Roman siege of Jerusalem and the wholesale slaughter of Jews during AD 66-70 – within the perspective of a universal event, because all nations would be at least indirectly affected. Luke 21:24 specifies of what this tribulation would consist: "And they shall fall by the edge of the sword, and shall be led away captive into all nations, and Jerusalem shall be trodden down of the Gentiles, until the time of the Gentiles be fulfilled." During the five years of the Jewish Wars, the Jews in Judea was almost exterminated.

The Jewish historian Josephus reported, "If the misfortunes which had befallen any nation from the beginning of the world were compared with those of the Jews, they would appear much inferior by comparison" (see also Dan. 12:1). In addition to Josephus' detailed and graphic accounts of the siege and fall of Jerusalem, Jesus also foretells massive violent Jewish destruction, especially in several passages in Luke.

On one occasion, certain Jews reasoned with Jesus about a number of Galileans who had been brutally slain by the Roman sword (Luke 13:1). Pilate had mingled their blood with his sacrifices, probably near the temple courts. Jesus perceived that the Jews thought that those Galileans must have been the most wicked and vile sinners in their district. But He told them flatly that their reasoning was false (v. 2b), and warned them that unless they repented they would experience a violent death (v.3). Fulfillment came when the Romans overran Jerusalem in AD 70.

Jesus next recounted the time when the huge stones of the tower of Siloam toppled upon eighteen people and crushed their bodies. These Jews were familiar with the tragedy. Said Christ, "Are you thinking that these died because of their extreme wicked living – above all others in Jerusalem? No! That is not why they died." He then promised them the same terrible physical destruction, unless they changed their hearts. Most of them did not repent, and similarly perished in the destruction of Jerusalem.

Immediately following these warnings of physical destruction, Jesus related the parable of the fig tree which consists of a man, who after planting a fig tree in his vineyard, earnestly looked for fruit on it, but would ultimately cut it down if it failed to yield (Luke 13:6-9). The application to the orthodox Jews of Jesus' generation is clear. For three years Jesus looked for fruits of repentance, but found none. Verse 8 indicates that additional gospel preaching would take place to change the hearts of the Jews. This effort saw fulfillment in the gospel preaching during the generation after the cross. Finally, in verse 9, if gospel fruit failed to materialize, the Jews could expect to die as violently as those certain Galileans and the people at Siloam. The obvious fulfillment occurred in AD 70, when the Jews were slaughtered en masse, set fire in houses, hurled over walls and from buildings, and were mangled by falling stones, and later piled together in the streets.

In Luke 19:41-44, Jesus wept and prophesied the tribulation and siege of AD 70. Amid the demonstrations of shouting of glad hosannahs of His followers, Jesus lamented over the wicked city that He knew would soon slay him. "If thou hadst known in this day, even thou, the things which belong unto peace! but now they are hid from thine eyes . . ." refers to God's era of opportunity and mercy accorded the Jews, but most were blinded by unbelief. By accepting Him and "the things which belong to peace," the rebellion against Rome would have been averted and the city left intact. The people would have gained both earthly and ultimately heavenly peace.

In verses 43-44, Jesus vividly described an ancient siege and promised that such days would come upon Jerusalem: "For the days shall come upon thee, when thine enemies shall cast up a bank about thee, and compass thee round, and keep thee in on every side, and shall dash thee to the ground, and the children within thee; and they shall not leave in thee one stone upon another; because thou knewest not the time of thy visitation." This "visitation" is divine inspection or examination (Greek *episkopay*), a "payday" (see Luke 19:15f).

In explicit fulfillment of Jesus' words, Roman legions first would encircle the city. Next, the soldiers would build a siege wall of earth and stone around it, thus sealing it off and preventing escape or reinforcement of the population inside. Siege banks, or ramparts, could then be thrown up and battering rams brought to bear upon the walls. It would be just a matter of time before conquest would be successful. Truly, it was the eleventh hour for the wayward Jewish nation. Once inside the city, the Romans would slay entire families.

Of the temple and associated buildings, not one of its stones would be left upon another (v. 44), something Jesus later would again foretell (Matt. 24:3). The end of the Jewish state resulted from internal social and religious moral decay, topped by the failure of legalistic Jews to perceive that Jesus was the Christ visiting them and bringing salvation. This rejection brought about destructive consequences, physically and spiritually.

In Luke 21:24, Luke announced how terrible the Jewish war would be: many would fall by the sword, others would be led away captive to all nations, and "Jerusalem shall be trodden down of the Gentiles, until the times of the gentiles be fulfilled." Here, the Greek word for "times" is *kairos* (opportunity) and not *chronos* which merely means a space of time. Some translations insert "strangers" in place of Gentiles.

In five years of fighting, a few hundred thousand of Jerusalem's sons perished (Josephus greatly exaggerates by saying 1.1 million) and tens of thousands of others were taken prisoner and dragged away into Gentile Roman provinces, eventually to die by the sword or by wild beasts in public theatres. Some were compelled to fight in troops against one another or experienced other miserable torments.

The Roman General Titus reserved the young Jews of remarkable stature and appearance for his triumphal march through Rome in the fall of 70, while other men were deported to Egypt for a lifetime of slavery in the mines. In these many ways, Jerusalem was "trodden down of the Gentiles," a term which emphasizes Rome's utter contempt for the Jews and the degree of oppression meted to God's former chosen race. Roman strangers would take possession of Jerusalem. The phrase "times of the gentiles" refers to the opportunity of the Romans to carry out their destructive mission.

Fulfillment of Luke 21:24 therefore took place in the generation of first century Jerusalem, and does not await an end time restoration of the Jewish state, such as the modern secular nation of Israel which does not contain a pure Jewish race, but is composed of people of mixed blood from many nations.

Thus, in Matthew 24:21, Jesus described the great tribulation as an unprecedented time when the first century Jewish race faced virtual extermination. Speculators who teach that the great tribulation will occur yet in the future, at the end of time, involve themselves in a built-in contradiction. The ". . . nor ever shall be" of verse 21 implies the occurrence of lesser tribulations after the "great" one. The millennialists also lack an adequate answer for Jesus' admonition to the disciples to flee into the mountains and to pray that their flight from tribulation would not have to be made in the winter or on the Sabbath.

Consistent with the context, the tribulation was fulfilled during the time of the Jewish Wars, AD 66-70, when Jerusalem under lengthy attack was "trodden down" (Luke 21:24). The inhabitants of Jerusalem besieged in the spring and summer of 70 underwent a terrible famine, but the faithful had departed long before the city experienced its final siege. God answered their prayers for an unimpaired flight because secular history records the successful escape of thousands of faithful messianic Jews to the province of Pella, a town in the Decapolis east of the Jordan River.

Josephus and the Great Tribulation

In stunning confirmation of Matthew 24:21, the contemporary Jewish historian Flavius Josephus described the horrors of the Roman siege of Jerusalem in the late spring and summer of the year 70. No one could leave the city. Nowhere was there corn, wheat, or barley to be seen, and there was wholesale ransacking of food storage places.

People tormented one another for even a morsel of food, as marauders roamed the narrow streets of the city. "If anyone still had flesh on their bones, they were deemed to have plenty of stores; if they were already reduced to skeletons, they were passed over. . . They snatched food from the fire while still uncooked and ate like wolves."

If partisans saw a locked door, they presumed that the occupants were having a meal. Instantly they would break down the door, rush in and even squeeze throats to force out morsels of food. Madmen "stuffed bitter vetch up the genital passages of their victims, and drove sharp stakes into their seats. . . to make them admit possession of one loaf or reveal the hiding place of even a single handful of barley." Others raked sewers and old dunghills and swallowed food particles found there.

As the famine intensified in Jerusalem that summer, entire families perished. A deep silence and a deathly darkness enveloped the city. While burying others, many fell dead themselves. Like crazed tomb-robbers, bandits broke into houses of the dead and underground chambers, stripped their bodies of possessions, and came out laughing. With grinning mouths and dry eyes, stronger people watched their neighbors fall dead in their tracks.

After there was no more room for burials in the city, corpses were hurled over the walls to the Romans. The surrounding valleys were soon heaped with the dead, and a putrid stream trickled from under the decomposing bodies. Josephus claimed he saw 600,000 pauper bodies thrown out of Jerusalem's gates.

Many who fled to the Romans were whipped and tormented and crucified in full view of everyone within the walls. As a grim joke, some were nailed up in awkward positions, after first being flogged and needlessly tortured, so deep was the soldiers' wrath and hatred of the Jews. Others rushed to the enemy with their bodies bloated by starvation, as if by dropsy; the Romans stuffed food into their empty bellies nonstop until they burst.

On one occasion when a deserter was caught picking through his excretia for gold coins (for he had swallowed them before leaving Jerusalem), a rumor spread that all deserters were arriving stuffed with gold. The Arabians, with the Syrians, under the Roman guards, then cut open the refugees and ransacked their bellies, Josephus wrote that in a single night nearly 2,000 were ripped up.

As the plight of Jerusalem worsened, the innumerable corpses piled here and there throughout the city emitted a pestilential stench. While making sorties, the Jewish soldiers had to trample on thousands of bodies of kinsmen lying unburied on the streets. With the famine penetrating deeply throughout the city, friends and members of households came to blows with one another, if something to eat was detected. Children pulled morsels of rotten food from the very mouths of their feeble fathers.

Like open-mouthed mad dogs, hapless desperadoes stumbled along the streets, hammering upon doors like drunken men; in their pitiful state, they often broke into the same house two and three times an hour. They sank their teeth into anything – even dirty belts and worn-out shoes, stalks of old hay, and also the leather from shields. People began to prey upon one another to discover where food was, tormenting friend and foe.

Much fighting broke out between warring Jewish factions, and thousands of the innocent were killed. Nothing was done for the wounded. Incredibly, rash party leaders set fire to storehouses of grain and other provisions, effectually robbing the city of food supplies dearly needed as the siege progressed. One plunderer resorted to sacrilege, melting down many of the sacred utensils which had been used in the temple.

Josephus tells of one mother, already robbed of everything by looters, who laid hand on her own baby. She reportedly said, "With the Romans there is only slavery, even if we are alive when they come; but famine is forestalling slavery, and the partisans [looters] are even crueller than either. Come, you must be food for me."

While she spoke she killed her son, then roasted him and ate one half, concealing the rest. Sniffing the unholy smell, the partisans reappeared and asked what was being prepared. The woman then reportedly said, "Help yourself, I've had my share." But the men went away quivering. The deed struck the entire city with horror, said the historian, and people were regarded as blessed who died before they had heard or seen such great evils.

Amid the din of Roman soldiers moving about and shouting while conquering the lower section of the city, the Jews even set fire to some of their own buildings. The aggressors moved fast, pilfering gold objects, money, clothing and other precious items from stores and houses. Every soldier became so laden with plunder that the value of gold was said to have fallen by one half.

With no pity or cry of emotion, they thrust their swords indiscriminately into any living enemy – even unarmed women, children, and feeble old men. Soon the ground could not be seen between the corpses. Stated Josephus with the usual exaggeration, "The whole city ran with blood, insomuch that many things which were burning were extinguished by the blood."

Since non–destruction of shrines and buildings of strength and grandeur was the general Roman custom in warfare, General Titus originally intended to starve the city into surrender and capture intact its glorious buildings as a trophy of victory. But the obstinacy of the Jewish soldiers compelled him to press on and systematically destroy the city, virtually house by house.

In the midst of the Roman advance, the Jews themselves torched the porticos of the great Jewish temple whose reconstruction had been completed by Herod less than ten years earlier. Another report says that Titus' soldiers, after setting fire to the halls around the temple, hurled a firebrand through the golden gate (window), causing the temple itself to burn. Amidst the General's explicit orders to extinguish the flames, his men instead pressed on with unrestrained violence and warlike vehemence and fury against the despised Jews. Soldiers vied with each other in the destruction, making the Jews feel the brunt of their unchained rage. Soon the entire structure was ablaze, illuminating the sky.

Historian Philip Schaff wrote significantly, "When the flames arose, the Jews raised a hideous yell and tried to put out the fire; while others, clinging with a last convulsive grasp to their messianic hopes, rested in the declaration of a false prophet, that God in the midst of the conflagration of the Temple would give a signal for the deliverance of his people" (*History of the Christian Church, Vol I*, p. 200).

To this description, Josephus added, "No one can conceive a louder, more terrible shriek than arose from all sides during the burning of the temple. The shout of victory and the jubilee of the legions sounded through the wailings of the people, now surrounded with fire and sword. . . increased the deafening roar. . . Yet the misery itself was more terrible than this disorder. This hill on which the temple stood was seething hot, but seemed enveloped to its base in one sheet of flame."

In a short time the gold on the roofs melted and flowed into the crevices and mortar joints and even to the foundation stones. A very short time later, Titus ordered these supporting stones beneath the temple to be broken up. In the sift for gold, most of them were dislodged, scraped off the site and thrown down. Only the temple platform remained standing, as did three towers as monuments to posterity of the strength of the city. The Romans spared part of the western wall as barracks for soldiers left there in garrison. Jesus' advance words about the fate of Herod's magnificent temple, "Not one stone would be left upon another" (Matt. 24:3), in principle, were fulfilled. Though the centerpiece of the nation Israel had been reduced, it took another three weeks of fighting to subdue the remaining upper part of the city.

Among the last buildings to be seized was Herod's Palace. There Jewish partisans sought refuge and slaughtered an estimated 8,400 kinsmen who had crowded into the building. Anyone on the streets and in houses quickly fell to the Romans, who found rooms piled high with the corpses of starvation. Other Jews hiding in the sewers were ferreted out, and the ground was torn up in search of enemies. They all died a violent death.

This Roman-inflicted suffering of Jerusalem and the bloody partisan strife is indeed the great tribulation that Jesus foretold in Matthew 24:21. The many incidents of hardship experienced by the besieged during the spring and summer of AD 70, as penned by Josephus, combine to form perhaps the most horrible picture of misery ever experienced by man. Nothing else on record matches the misery, the violence, the savageness, and wanton destruction of the Jewish Wars, making Jerusalem a veritable hell on earth.

The confusion, the madness of howling Jewish partisans, the merciless Roman siege which brought famine, starvation of fearful proportions, pestilence, despair, the fighting among and within Jewish families and the murder and rape by the enraged and hate-filled Roman soldiery – all of these things together brought about the bloodiest and cruelest war in history. Even if only half of what the fertile imagination of Josephus recorded was true, the tribulation upon Jerusalem was still horrible enough.

Soon afterwards, Josephus described the city: "No one – not even a foreigner – who had seen the. . . glorious suburbs of the city, and now set eyes on her present desolation, could have helped sighing and groaning at so terrible a change; for every trace of beauty had been blotted out by the war, and nobody who had known it in the past and came upon it suddenly would have recognized the place: when he was already there, he would have been still looking for the city."

The desolation was so complete that one Eleazer said to his countrymen: "What is become of our city, which was believed to be inhabited by God? It is rooted up from the very foundations, and the only monument of it that is left, is the camp of those who destroyed it, still pitched upon its remains. Some unhappy old men sit over the ashes of the temple, and a few women reserved by the enemy for the basest of injuries."

Thus ended the war against Jerusalem, though Masada and two other Jewish fortresses were yet to be conquered. Temple vessels and other implements were collected for transport to Rome, signifying the finality of Israel and its religious system. Indeed, they had experienced "the great tribulation" of Matthew 24:21 and the "days of vengeance, that all things which are written may be fulfilled" (Luke 21:22).

Therefore, no other prophecies concerning the nation of Israel and promises of future regathering or conversion of the Jews, remain to be fulfilled. Rather, all that Jesus said about these things, as recorded in Matthew 24, was explicitly realized in the events associated with first century Judea and the instrument of God's wrath, the Roman armies.

Chapter Nine

THE GREAT TRIBULATION —
CONTINUED

MATTHEW 24:21, which prophesied the unprecedented tribulation that would come upon the Jews, covers the entire period of the Jewish Wars, AD 66-70. In Jerusalem there were wholesale killings through internal strife and shortages of food. The Roman invaders demolished the city's magnificent buildings, hurled bodies from towers and walls, crucified many others, plundered and slayed thousands in the streets and in houses and led untold others into captivity.

Concerning that time, Jesus said, "Except these days be shortened, no *flesh* would be saved" (v. 22). The "days" include the several occasions of Jewish faction fighting and the occasions in the Jewish Wars when Jerusalem was besieged by the Romans and the Idumaeans. As the Jews are the subject of the discourse, this verse declares that lengthy sieges would have indiscriminately exterminated both messianic Jews and unbelievers, people living in the mid-first century in Judea, even as *all flesh* in Isaiah 66:15-16 is not universal but confined to the Jewish nation of 740-710 B.C. which had left God for idol worship. Now, in Matthew 24:22, Jesus describes the judgment of the Jewish nation in AD 70, with the attendant tragic consequences of suffering and tribulation upon all flesh in Jerusalem.

Since the Romans would slaughter all, Jesus adds, "but for the elect sake those days shall be shortened" (v. 22b). The providential opportunity for messianic Jews to flee to safety would not have been possible, except that the days of siege and tribulation by the Romans in AD 66 and the Idumaeans two years later be limited. On one hand was the fury of Jewish Zealots in Jerusalem, and on the other the hatred of the bloodthirsty Roman and Idumaean armies during the tribulation. God Himself saw that the period of misery and suffering would extend only certain lengths of time, so that Christian Jews might be able to flee from the city.

At this point Luke adds significantly, "For these must be days of vengeance, that all things which are written may be fulfilled" (21:22). Now the calamities foretold by Moses, Joel, Daniel, and other Jewish prophets, as well as Jesus' own words, would come to pass with aggravation upon the disobedient nation.

The period of divine retribution and punishment is reminiscent of Israel in 750-725 B.C. In that early era Hosea preached about the consequences of religious corruption and rebellion against God: "The days of visitation [vengeance] are come, the days of recompense are come; Israel should know it . . . for the abundance of thine iniquity, and because the enmity is great" (9:7).

In both Hosea and Luke, the "days of vengeance" is a period of penal visitation upon Israel, for wicked people had made the nation ripe for judgment. Now in the mid–first century, tribulation and punishment by military forces would come upon Judea. In a judgment of the distant past (about 721 B.C.), God had raised up the Assyrians to conquer idolatrous, unfaithful Israel (Isa. 7:17), while against Judea nearly 800 years later Christ, as ruler of the kings of the earth, would come upon the Jews of Jerusalem, using the Roman armies as the instrument of His vengeance.

Matthew 24:22 began to be fulfilled during a Jewish rebellion against Rome in April of the year 66, occasioned by the theft of funds from the temple treasury by the Roman Judean procurator, the unprincipled, tyrannical Gessius Florus. The act provoked a Jewish rebellion, one of many over the past few decades, but this one affected religious sensitivities. In response, some Jews ridiculed the procurator's greed by feigning the collection of donations for "poor, unfortunate Florus." In response to this mockery, Florus sent into Jerusalem a detachment of troops which sacked part of the city and scourged and even crucified a great many of the most honorable Jews seized at random.

The masses in Jerusalem ultimately prevailed, however, and Florus withdrew to Caeserea. King Agrippa exhorted the people to return to obedience to the emperor, and order was restored in Jerusalem. Meanwhile, radical Jews began to occupy the Masada fortress overlooking the Dead Sea. They persuaded certain temple officials to suspend the daily sacrifice for the emperor and accept no more sacrifices from the Gentiles, actions tantamount to an open declaration of revolt against the Romans. Such rebellion was still another example of repeated outbreaks among the Jews in the middle of the decade of AD 60, a period of swift decline in the holy city.

These rebels had gained the upper hand in Jerusalem over the chief priests and others of nobility, including the supporters of King Agrippa. The two factions each controlled part of the city, and numerous conflicts raged. In one fight, the Zealots torched the palaces of the high priest and of Agrippa. They also laid siege to Herod's Palace, also setting it on fire. To crown their victory, the rebels murdered several people, including the high priest. Bloody battles also ensued between Jews and Gentiles in other Judean cities.

After long delay and preparation, the Governor of Syria, Cestius Gallus, took steps to put down the disturbances in

Judea. With the Roman 12th legion, as well as auxiliary cavalry, cohorts, and men supplied by Agrippa and others, Gallus marched upon Jerusalem from the west, arriving in October 66, and pitched camp on Mount Scopus. He soon occupied the suburb of Bezetha, but when he failed in his assault on the temple mount, Gallus seemingly inexplicably retreated.

God's providence evidently intervened. Josephus said of Cestius: "If he had chosen at that very hour to force his way inside the walls, the city would have been his immediately and the war brought to an end." But several officers may have accepted bribes from one of the leaders of a Jewish sect to turn him from the attempt. The Jewish army did score victories over the retreating Romans, which left valuable war equipment and material before escaping to Antioch. With great jubilation, the victors returned to Jerusalem in October 66.

Josephus concluded: "If only he [Cestius] had persevered with the siege a little longer, he would have captured the city at once; but. . . flying in the face of all reason, [he] retired from the city. [He] suddenly called off his men, abandoning hope, though he had suffered no reverse."

As the Romans retreated from Judea, Jewish followers of Christ left because they knew that the great legions would return at any time – her desolation was "at hand." (When Jesus announced that the kingdom of God was "at hand" in Mark 1:15, fulfillment came only several months later in the power displayed in Jesus' miracles and those of the disciples and – less than three years later – in the sending of the Holy Spirit among God's spiritual assembly of believers, the *ekklesia* of Christ).

Seeing the Roman activity, Jewish believers were then given the opportunity to heed Jesus' instruction to flee to the mountains (Matt. 24:16), because the city soon would be besieged again. For these would be the days when Jesus would be meting out justice, "that all things which are written may be fulfilled" (Luke 21:22; see also Jer. 46:10). These writings were scrolls of the Hebrew prophets – Moses, Isaiah, Daniel, etc. Also, the disciples would recall Jesus' actual utterances of these prophecies then freely circulating as authentic oral tradition, words later recorded in scripture. Josephus declared that after the departure of Cestius Gallus, "many prominent Jews fled from the city like swimmers from a sinking ship."

As the city of Jerusalem entered the year 67, pacifists were swept along by the reality that the Romans would again attack very soon. The inveterate pro-Roman sympathizers left the city for good. Either by force or persuasion, the rebels organized for military action, not only the citizens of Judea but also in all other eleven political divisions of Judea. Galilee was put under the charge of Josephus, the future historian.

The appointment of Josephus to the vital Galilean command reflected his prominent position within Judea's aristocratic society. A man with only a religious education suddenly had to organize untrained Galileans to fight the seasoned Romans. But within Galilee a daring reckless partisan filled with burning hatred for the Romans, John of Gischala, would not submit to Josephus, wishing to fight Rome to the bitter end. John unsuccessfully tried to have Josephus dismissed.

AD 67 – The War in Galilee

During the winter of 66-67, the citizens of Jerusalem readied themselves for the inevitable return of the Romans. Walls and buildings were reinforced, and even young boys were trained in the use of weapons. War materials of every kind were stockpiled in vacant rooms.

Emperor Nero was sojourning in Greece when he learned of the defeat of Cestius. Now the task of subduing the Jewish revolt was placed in the hands of the experienced Vespasian, who that very winter began to make preparations for a Judean campaign. In Antioch he marshalled an army of two legions which was soon joined by the 15th legion under his son, Titus – in all, about 60,000 men.

Soon the Romans conquered all of the Judean lowlands and most of Galilee, but not the fortress at Tiberius. Vespasian had to resort to a regular siege, and Josephus (not a true general) countered with minor tricks and stratagems to keep the Romans off guard. He left the impression that there was no water shortage in the fortress by having clothes dripping with water hung on the battlements. He insured the continuance of food supplies by dressing his people in skins and sending them out at night to creep past the Roman sentries.

At other times he ingeniously destroyed assault ramps and battering rams, pouring boiling mixtures of oil on them, as well as on the soldiers. Nevertheless, this important outpost fell into Roman hands in June of 68, and Josephus himself surrendered. Brought before Vespasian, Josephus assumed the role of a prophet by telling the general of his ultimate ascendancy to the emperorship. Finally by the fall of 67, Vespasian had mastered all of Galilee, including the town of Gischala, but the local leader, John, along with his band of Zealots, escaped the night before its capture and fled to Jerusalem.

AD 68-69 – The Siege of Jerusalem

Even in the face of constant Roman military threat, factions within Jerusalem continued their infighting, which resulted in much bloodshed. The head of the fanatical Zealots or nationalists, John of Gischala, murdered some of Jerusalem's prominent citizens and any pro-Roman sympathizers he found. Another man just as intolerant of authority, Simon Bar-Giora, assembled a band of followers to loot and devastate southern Palestine. He later vied with John for control of Jerusalem.

To obtain support against the prominent and respected of Jerusalem, the Zealots urged the warlike Idumaeans to join them, under the pretext that the ruling party in Judea was surreptitiously in league with the Romans. For a long

ROMAN CATAPULT.

THE BATTERING RAM.

while the Idumaeans remained encamped around the city; then during a fierce storm the Zealots managed to open the city gates to their allies, who robbed and murdered people not aligned with the Zealots. After one night of fighting, the rising sun greeted 8,500 corpses. Among the victims was the high priest Ananus, felled after a mock trial. Stated Josephus, "The death of Ananus marked the time of the eventual overthrow of the city."

It was about this time, if not earlier, that the fugitive Christian community of Jerusalem fled "as a result of divine guidance" and resettled in Pella, a free Gentile city in the Decapolis which enjoyed many natural advantages. Pella was at peace amid Roman military campaigns. There the messianic Jews lived on savings; an unsubstantiated tradition says that God miraculously fed them.

What accounts for these withdrawals, first by the Romans, and then by the Idumaeans? Was God protecting His people? Twice the city had been surrounded by enemies, and each time external events prevented its capture. Truly, as verse 22 states, the days were cut short for the sake of the elect so that they could flee, fulfilling Christ's explicit words, for only the fainthearted would be trapped with the rebellious and corrupt Jews when the city again would be encircled by foreign armies.

God used natural means to provide an escape for His people, a fulfillment of God's promise recorded by Daniel: " . . . There shall be a time of trouble such as never was, since there was a nation, even to that same time: and at that time thy people shall be delivered" (12:1). Joel prophesied of the same event that "there shall be those that escape," adding "whoever shall call upon the name of Jehovah shall be delivered" (2:32). King Jesus intervened in behalf of His covenant faithful in Jerusalem, who prayed for relief and meditated on His words. Yet, the necessity of inflicting vengeance upon the disobedient generation of Jews had to be fulfilled, and that part of God's plan continued.

Meanwhile, Vespasian and his generals differed on how to conquer Jerusalem. The latter thought that the city could be taken with ease, because of the infighting, while Vespasian wanted the internal struggle to allow itself full vent. With the arrival of better weather in the spring of 68, Vespasian roamed the countryside, burning towns and farms and slaughtering civilians and any Jewish army unit he encountered. Forests were stripped bare, and ground long under cultivation of plants and vegetables was trampled so heavily that it was thereafter harder to work than barren soil.

The country was now sufficiently subjugated for the siege of the capital to begin. In Caeserea, Vespasian had just started preparations when news came early in June that Nero had met a violent end. The general postponed his expedition against Jerusalem, waiting anxiously to see who would replace Nero as emperor.

Now the Judean situation suddenly changed. Because of uncertainties about the future of the empire, Vespasian suspended all military projects, pending receipt of a new directive from Rome. After news came early in the winter of AD 68-69 that Galba had been elevated to the throne, Vespasian sent his son Titus to Rome to pay homage to the new emperor. But when Galba was assassinated in January of 69, Titus returned to Caeserea, where his father had been playing a waiting game. Anxious for the safety of the empire, Vespasian did not want to waste time and energy pursuing the war against the Jews. Soon Otho ascended the emperorship.

By May and June of 69, after allowing a full year to pass without military operations, Vespasian was again conquering towns on the approaches to Jerusalem from both north and south. Meanwhile, the Jewish factions in the city committed every imaginable crime, butchering their captives even in broad daylight, as if they were herds of unclean animals. Houses were plundered and people killed on sight. Josephus reported, "The Dead Sea too was filled with corpses, which the [Jordan] river carried down to it by the thousands."

In Rome, emperor Otho lasted less than three months and was succeeded by Vitellius. Instability reigned in Rome and everything was in a melting pot. Keeping an eye on Rome's uncertain politics, Vespasian was distracted from the war against the Jews. By July 1, Vespasian himself was acclaimed emperor in Egypt, and within two weeks was thus recognized throughout the entire eastern Roman Empire. Now political matters vied for his attention with prosecuting the war against the Judean rebels. He sent a trusted general to Rome with an army on his behalf, but Vespasian himself stayed in Alexandria.

During his residence there, he learned that his cause in Rome had triumphed, and that Vitellius had been knifed. Late in AD 69, Vespasian became the fifth Roman ruler within thirty months. The instability amply fulfills Matthew 24:6-7, "And ye shall hear of wars and rumors of wars. . . For nation shall rise against nation" – a definite sign preceding the destruction of Jerusalem. Any discerning disciple of Christ still in the city would surely not delay a departure.

Meanwhile, in Jerusalem, internal disruption had grown worse. Now three major parties locked in ceaseless fighting turned the city into a continual battlefield. Once Titus' armies would beset the city, there would be no possibility of escape, even as Jesus Himself said, "The days shall come upon thee, that thine enemies shall cast a trench about thee, and compass thee around, and keep thee on every side" (Luke 19:43).

AD 70 – The Siege and Capture of Jerusalem

With his supremacy in Rome firmly established in the winter of 69-70, Vespasian (though still residing in Alexandria) again turned his attention eastward to the Judean campaign. He then sent his son, Titus, with four legions together with numerous contingents of allied kings, to lay siege to Jerusalem. In all, Titus' main force in Caeserea early in the year 70 consisted of about 80,000 men. Soon he was on the upward march toward Jerusalem, reaching the walls of the holy city only days before the Passover in April.

Even as the Romans stood before the city gates devising strategy, the fighting between the parties within still had not abated. When one partisan leader opened the gates of the temple forecourt to the festival visitors, John of Gischala exploited the moment by smuggling in additional heavily armed men. Another bloodbath occurred, and John reigned supreme within the troubled city. Incidental delays in military activity to allow Christians additional opportunities to escape to safety were now over.

The siege by Titus was about to begin against Jerusalem, a city built on perhaps as many as three hills, the most southerly being a higher western one (Mount Zion, in the "upper city") and a lower ridge to the east (Hill Ophel), divided by a deep north-south ravine, the Tyropoeon. A northerly extension of the Ophel ridge was Mount Moriah, the seat of the enlarged temple of Herod the Great. On the hump-like Hill Acra even

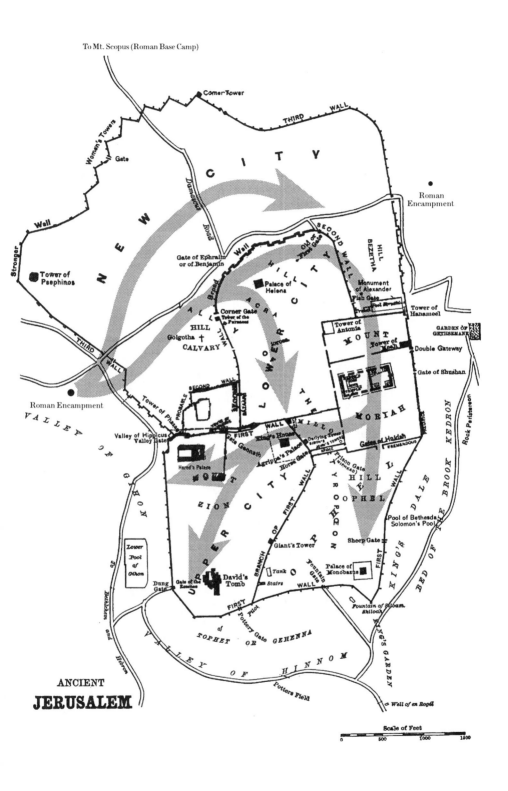

To Mt. Scopus (Roman Base Camp)

ANCIENT
JERUSALEM

further northwest, Antiochus Epiphanes had built a fortress in about 165 B.C.

Adjacent to the temple's north side was the strong Antonia fortress, built fifty cubits high on a rocky saddle between the temple mount and Hill Bezetha, of "new city." It contained broad courts, baths, and a magnificent palace. Its highest tower had a commanding view of the temple. A deep trench divided the Antonia from the suburb of Bezetha.

The temple itself was contained within four strong walls of perfectly bonded stones, and itself constituted an imposing fortress. The building of Solomon's temple earlier on the same site is described in I Kings 6. Jerusalem's upper and lower cities also were enclosed by a sweeping common wall tangent to the temple's western wall. Still another wall adjacent to Jerusalem on its north side separated a recently completed third wall, which in a northerly sweep enclosed the "new city" of Bezetha, partially built on a high hill of the same name. Hill Calvary was located in the "new city," just outside of Jerusalem's walls (Heb. 13:12, John 19:17-20).

With two legions encamped on nearby Mount Scopus, seven furlongs (just less than a mile) north of Jerusalem, Titus directed his offensive against Jerusalem's northwestern side; one legion had pitched camp on the west side, while still another legion was stationed just beyond the east wall of the "new city." Powerful battering rams began their work in three places, with one of them finally breaking through the third wall on May 25. But the now-joined forces of the Jews nearly undermined the Roman engines of war, by a sustained fire of javelins, darts and stones upon the aggressors.

Soon the Romans began their assault on the second wall, gaining control of it before the end of May. Now Titus could press his attack on the lower city and the tower of Antonia. After sufficient timber had been hauled in by wagons from forests four and a half hours away, each of the four Roman legions built a new rampart to try to subdue Antonia. Battering rams began beating against the tower walls made of smooth flagstone, but it took a contingent of skilled wall scalers until the end of July to capture the Antonia. As the Romans quickly razed the tower to the ground, Jewish soldiers retreated into the temple zone.

Now in control of the lower city, Titus made preparations for a full-scale attack on the stout-walled temple itself. Until about that time, the daily morning and evening sacrifices continued to be offered, finally being suspended around August 1 because temple workers were needed for defense. Once again, four ramparts were erected of building materials imported from afar.

Early in August, after construction of assault ramps was finished, the siege of the temple began. But the batterers could not inflict even the slightest damage upon the gigantic temple walls. Titus then decided to fire the gates to open a way for his soldiers to storm the outer temple court. In a council of war on August 27, Titus announced that he wished to spare the temple. Within a day, the Jews mounted two forceful counterattacks from the inner forecourt. In repelling these, a soldier threw a firebrand into the temple proper.

Soon the resplendent building was ablaze. The Zealots managed to flee into the as yet unconquered upper city, the only sanctuary available to them. General Titus called upon Simon and John to capitulate, but since they would not surrender unconditionally, the Romans ferociously pressed their attack. As the Romans advanced, they butchered all who fell into their hands, the aged and children alike, systematically robbing every house.

With no prospect of a voluntary surrender, the Roman soldiers again erected ramparts next to fortified places, and the battering rams soon breached the walls of the upper city. The soldiers entered with little difficulty, since the Jews could not longer offer serious resistance. The Romans set up military standards and sang hymns of victory. On September 26, after more than five months of fighting, the entire city was in the hands of the victors.

Sons of Jerusalem who had not fallen victim to the famine or sword were sent to the Egyptian mines or to Rome for gladiatorial combat. Several hundred of the handsomest and strongest men, including the tireless rebels, John and Simon, were reserved for the march of triumph in Rome early in aD 71. Both men were imprisoned for life. Titus celebrated the hard-won victory with eulogies addressed to his army. Rewards were bestowed for outstanding acts of valor amid sacrifices of thanksgiving and a festive banquet in Caeserea.

AD 70-74 – The Sequel to the War

With one legion remaining in Jerusalem as garrison, Titus deposited booty and placed prisoners in custody at Caeserea. Some of the Jews were forced to take part in fights with wild animals and in other gladiatorial games. Throughout Palestine northward to Antioch, Titus celebrated his victory in various cities and towns with spectacles in which Jewish prisoners killed each other in combat.

Nevertheless, parts of Palestine were not yet subdued – Masada and two other fortresses. By the year 74 only Masada still held out in spite of a long investment. The city was built on a mountain so high and precipitous that it was impossible to encounter it with siege instruments. After elaborate preparations, a huge dirt rampart was built on its west side to allow the approach of a battering ram toward the wall.

Finally, the Romans breached the seemingly impregnable wall, only to find a hastily built wood and earthen barrier behind it which the soldiers soon destroyed by fire. When the Jews realized that no hope of further resistance remained, the leaders successfully carried out a mass suicide the night before the Romans set foot inside Masada. Thus, the last Jewish bastion had been taken in April 74, and Judea's fate had been permanently sealed.

Chapter Ten

THE EAGLES AND
THE CARCASS

WHEN THE YEAR 70 DAWNED, Judea had experienced four years of warfare, including two attempts by the Romans to capture Jerusalem. In the spring of that year the Romans under General Titus began to march upon Jerusalem to encircle it until effecting a surrender. He would establish three base camps to quarter more than 80,000 troops who were only eager to engage the despised, rebellious Jews.

Meanwhile, during the same four years, warring factions in the city turned it into "a battlefield for those plotters and their disreputable followers, and between them the people were being torn to bits like a great carcass," in the words of Josephus. The infighting hamstrung the military effort against the Romans. Still, Titus needed the entire summer to subdue the city. His siege, the very heart of Matthew's "great tribulation" (24:21), was much longer than Cestius' in AD 66, or the Idumaeans' two years later. Trade with other cities and provinces virtually stopped.

The Rise of False Christs

Matthew 24:23-26 tells how false christs, indefinitely introduced in verse 5, would appear before and during the attacks upon Jerusalem: "Then, if any man shall say unto you, 'Lo, here is the Christ,' or, 'Here,' believe it not. For there shall arise false christs, and false prophets, and shall show great signs and wonders; so as to lead astray, if possible, even the elect. Behold, I have told you beforehand. If therefore they shall say unto you, 'Behold, he is in the wilderness,' go not forth: 'Behold, he is in the inner chambers,' believe it not."

The word "then" in verse 23 links the impostors with the time of the siege of Jerusalem of verse 21. Pretending to be God-sent and claiming the title of Messiah, they would feign miracles and impose fraudulent signs and wonders among their countrymen, just as pseudo-prophets misled others during national misfortunes previously. Many deceivers and pretenders had appeared at the time of the previous siege of Jerusalem in 586 B.C. (Jer. 23:9-32, Ezek. 22:25-31).

Specifically, the false christs could either be fake prophets, who would stay secluded in wilderness areas or in secret chambers in Jerusalem before and during the siege of AD 70, or alleged reported appearances of God's true Christ promising physical deliverance from the Romans. Amid times of great unrest and misery, rumors might naturally circulate that He had come. Faithful disciples (II Tim. 3:9) could discriminate between the genuine and the spurious, who might use Christ's very words while imposing signs and wonders.

Since in times of distress man is generally inclined to place trust in the marvelous and the astonishing, impostors preyed upon the weak and the gullible among the Jews and the Samaritans. According to Eusebius and Jerome, one Jewish deceiver, Barcochebus (whose name meant "son of a star"), pretended to vomit flames. He styled himself as having come down out of heaven to the Jews to bring them light amid their misfortunes. Josephus wrote that during the siege one false prophet persuaded 6000 people to enter the temple to see signs of deliverance, and all of them perished. Jesus had foretold the presence of false leaders, appearing in secret temple chambers as well as in the deserts (v. 26).

In about AD 69, one weaver of deliverance promised to show signs and apparitions, but his followers were captured by Vespasian, who imprisoned or slew them or burned them alive. Josephus also related another incident where counterfeit prophets persuaded many to follow them into the wilderness, where the impostors promised the cessation of all evil through "divine inspiration."

Still another pseudo-prophet assured desperate Jews deliverance from the Roman soldiers, even as they were about to capture the temple in the summer of AD 70. He said that in the temple they would receive miraculous signs. Instead, when the Romans set the temple on fire, all of them perished in the flames, or plunged to their deaths to escape them. In contrast, God's Christ, Jesus of Nazareth, possessed all of the qualities of simplicity and truth (I Peter 2:22). His credentials were the many miracles wrought by his hands, something which Isaiah may have foretold in the ministries of John the Baptist and Christ (35:3-10), though John himself performed no miracles.

Verse 27 declares that the coming of the Son of man would be as a lightning flash: "For as the lightning cometh forth from the east and is seen even unto the west; so shall be the coming of the son of man." Thus His presence would be felt all over. The "coming" is a presence, as in verse 24:3, denoting Jesus' divine visitation, which was fulfilled in the approach of the Roman armies and the capture of the city. Lightning denotes swift demonstration of power, pointing to the suddenness of events prior to Jerusalem's destruction.

Once again, Jesus employed apocalyptic language in Jewish prophetic style, even as Isaiah did in describing a victory by Yahweh over Assyria (30:30-31). In Zechariah 9:14, Jehovah's influence would go forth as lightning. The coming of the Son of man (v. 27) similarly pointed to a temporal judgment, this time of corrupt Jerusalem in AD 70.

In contrast with the false prophets, Christ would not come in secret, but His power would be displayed as openly as lightning flashes. Far from a localized presence as in the desert or in the temple, Jesus' influence would extend from east to west, beyond the horizons.

So now, God's saints would no longer look for a redeemer within Judea only, but the power and royal rule of Christ would influence people even in the utmost parts of the known world, something only the Son of man could do. In coming in vengeance against the wicked nation, Judea, Christ would be manifesting the power of His kingdom.

The phrase "coming of the Son of man" in verse 27 is rendered in Luke 17:24, "so shall the Son of man be in His day." These parallel statements show Christ to be present in vengeance against His Jewish contemporaries—of *that* generation—as emphatically stated in Luke 17:25. Between Matthew's verses 27 and 28, Luke inserts additional remarks about the suddenness of destruction and calamity. The narratives reunite at Matthew 24:28 and Luke 17:37, both of which tell of the eagles and the carcass.

Luke 17:26-36 furnishes two illustrations that explain how it would be when the Son of man is revealed. (This "revealing" coincides with His "coming".) It would be as in Noah's time and as in the days of Lot. Rather than a description of conditions on earth at this coming, these stories demonstrate the *unexpectedness* of His coming. Warnings would go unheeded. (The Noah story is also in Matthew 24:37-38.)

Luke 17:31 admonishes people "in that day" – the hour of tribulation when the Son of man is revealed – to leave the city in haste, without delay: those on housetops should not retrieve goods in the house before fleeing, and field hands should likewise not return to their houses. (These admonitions also are in Matthew 24:17). See also Chapter Seven. When they heard that the Roman battalions were in full march, there was no time for extensive packing of goods and raiment. Constant vigilance was essential (Matt. 24:42-44), for temporal objects should be of little concern when personal safety had to be secured at any price.

Luke 17:34-36 tells of the calamities which would transpire at the revelation of the Son of man: God's taking of one man from two in a bed, one woman from two grinding together, and one man from two field workers (see also Matt. 24:40-41). Thus, the faithful disciple who believed Jesus' warnings recognized the signs and fled to safety in the mountains east of the Jordan River, while the unbelieving Jew beside him perished in the siege.

And so, one person providentially escaped by adhering to Christ's words of warning to flee, while the *unbeliever* was taken for slaughter or captivity, coinciding with Christ's actions of gathering wheat while destroying chaff, as expressed in Matthew 3:12. These incidents which occurred just before AD 70, are contradicted by the modern premillennial reign theory, in which the *believer* is taken from the earth.

The Eagles and the Carcass

The proverb in Matthew 24:28, and its parallel in Luke 17:37, "Wheresoever the carcass (body) is, there will the eagles be gathered together," climaxes the thought of the several preceding verses in both gospel accounts. The image is of an enemy falling on its victim, alluding to the ancient statement, "Where the body of an animal falls, there would the eagles be found scenting it from afar."

As the fiercest bird of prey, the magnificent eagle can swoop down with incredible speed upon its victim. Its eyes see carrion from fantastic heights and distances. Its strength and rapacity tear victims apart. To demonstrate the swiftness and power and fierce cruelty of the Babylonians, the prophets employed the eagle as a fitting emblem of Israel and Judah's enemies. The eagle in Ezekiel 17:3 denotes Babylon as a nation of large dominion; similarly Moses told of Israel's enemy as a nation of fierce countenance that as an eagle would come from afar (Deut. 28:49).

Isaiah 46:11 refers to Cyrus, the Persian who conquered Babylon, as a carrion-eater: ". . . calling a ravenous bird from the east, the man that executeth my counsel from a far country." God is directly responsible for such judgments, as stated by Habakkuk 1:6-8: "For, lo, I raise up the Chaldeans, that bitter and hasty nation . . . Their horses also are swifter than leopards, and are more fierce than the evening wolves; and their horsemen press proudly on: yea their horsemen come from afar; they fly as an eagle that hasteth to devour." The *Commentary on Habakkuk* in the Dead Sea Scrolls applies this verse to Kittim (Rome), which would trample the earth and devour all the peoples [the Jews].

Earlier, the Assyrians would invade Israel, coming "as an eagle . . . against the house of Jehovah, because they have transgressed my covenant" (Hos. 8:1). Jeremiah referred to the backslidden people of Judah in 7:33: "And their dead bodies [carcasses] of this people shall be food for the birds [eagles] of the heavens." When Jerusalem and Judea would fall by the sword to their enemy, Babylon, God would give their carcasses for food for the birds of the heavens (Jer. 19:7; see also 4:13, 48:40; Lam. 4:19).

In Matthew 24:28, the eagles are the Roman legions and the city of Jerusalem is the carcass fit to be devoured. The apocryphal book *II Esdras* equates a powerful eagle with the kingdom of Rome (11:1-12:21). The figurative language is appropriate, for the nation was empty and spiritually dead. It was desolate (Matt. 23:38) and doomed to messianic destruction. Thus, where the carcass was situated, Christ would come in vengeance. It is a coming through the Roman army in judgment upon the evil Jewish people and corrupt religion.

In the summer of 70 and from an immense distance, the Romans literally "swarmed" like a multitude of eagles over

THOUGH THOU SHOULD MAKE THY NEST
AS HIGH AS THE EAGLE – JER. 49:16

decadent Judea to loot and devastate the land. Every major city was affected. In ancient times the Jewish nation had enjoyed God's protection and providential care, and the eagle exemplified these things. God had carried the Israelites out of Egypt on eagles' wings (Ex. 19:4, Deut. 32:11; see also Isa. 40:31).

Since the Jews and the Greeks did not distinguish between eagles and vultures, calling both by the generic term "eagle," some scholars say that the proper bird of Matthew 24:28 is carrion-kites, a species of vulture. But eagles will consume dead meat, whenever they detect it. Job declared that the eagle "dwelleth on the cliff. . . From thence she seeketh the prey, and her eyes behold afar off. Her young ones also suck up blood, and where the slain are, there she is" (39:27-30). The last phrase is similar to Matthew 24:28: Where the slain [carcasses] are, there is she [the eagle].

By the time of AD 66-70, Jerusalem, as well as the entire Jewish society and its religious life, was but a putrid corpse fit for removal suddenly and efficiently, as an eagle pounces upon a victim. In utter surprise the disciples ask, "Where, Lord?" (Luke 17:37). They wanted to know the location of the calamities of Matthew 24:22-28 and Luke 17:22-36. They were astonished, as if saying, "Surely not in Jerusalem of Judea!"

By identification of the carcass, the disciples' question would be answered. They would then understand why the powerful eagle would hastily fly there, for destruction was certain. Verily, the voracious eagles (the Roman armies) seemingly from out of nowhere spotted the prey, swooped down, tore and devoured the victim (Jerusalem), and flew away, leaving nothing but slick white bones. Indeed, as a putrid carcass attracts the eagle, so will moral and religious corruption be answered by divine judgment.

Chapter Eleven

THE STARS FALL. . .
THE HEAVENS SHAKE

THROUGHOUT SCRIPTURE, the end of the Jewish nation is emphasized in many highly figurative passages. It was Jesus Christ who "came" against the apostate nation Israel, wielding the iron rod of His wrath (Psa. 2:9, Rev. 1:5, 12:5, 19:15). This spiritual quality of Christ is expressed in figurative terms, using lightning, the clouds, various celestial objects, as found in the writings of Joel (2:28f) and other prophets.

Similarly, Matthew 24:29 also employs ominous words of calamity and doom: "But immediately after the tribulation of those days [see. v. 21], the sun shall be darkened, and the moon shall not give her light, and the stars shall fall from heaven, and the powers of the heavens shall be shaken. . ." Mark reads, "The powers that are *in* the heavens shall be shaken [dislocated]" (13:25). The imagery indicates an important turning point in history, but not an end of time event, as the premillennialists believe.

Rather than a yet-future "second coming," these verses announce something that would be fulfilled "immediately" after the events of verse 28 and those preceding it—the tribulation of Jerusalem and the capture of the city by the Romans. No length of time separates verses 28 and 29. Matthew is not saying that, after the tribulation upon Jerusalem has passed, then, after an indefinite interval of at least 1900 years, a great consummation would suddenly descend upon mankind.

Instead, the phraseology of verse 29 appropriately announces the end of Jewish institutional power in AD 70 and signifies the distress accompanying the destruction of Jerusalem in the very near future. Matthew's use of the sun, moon, stars, and the heavens is heavily indebted to longstanding Jewish prophetic imagery and key words which unmistakably describe temporal judgments of various ancient earthly societies, from 800 to about 500 B.C.

Isaiah 13:10 states that, "For the stars of heaven and the constellations thereof shall not give their light: the sun shall be darkened in its going forth, and the moon shall not cause its light to shine." This darkened sun, lightless moon and stars, and a shaking or a trembling of the heavens, all signified the end of Babylon's political leadership in the fifth century B.C. (see also v. 13). Assuredly, the prophet describes a local judgment—"the oracle of Babylon" (v. 1)—and therefore the context has no reference to yet future end time events.

Similarly, the fall of Edom and allied nations long ago was described as when "all the host of heaven shall be dissolved, and the heavens shall be rolled together as a scroll: and all their host shall fade away, as the leaf fadeth from the vine. . ." (Isa. 34:4). In this figure of judgment, several earthly governments ceased existence. Fulfillment before 700 B.C. is a matter of historical fact.

Jeremiah mixed heavenly signs with earthly ones to depict in his day, 600 B.C., a looming judgment of Jerusalem: "I beheld the earth, and lo, it was waste and void; and the heavens, and they had no light. I beheld the mountains, and lo, they trembled, and all the hills moved to and fro. . . . for thus, sayeth Jehovah, the whole land shall be a desolation, yet will I not make a full end. For this shall the earth mourn and the heavens above be black; because I have spoken it" (4:23-24, 27-28). The prophet tells about the end of Jerusalem's godlessness in 586 B.C. by the conquering nation Babylon, and not at the end of the world yet future, since at that time the people would not be brought to a *full* end.

Earlier, the prophet Joel, in about 830 B.C., emphasized the terribleness of God's visitation upon Judah, by associating the day of Jehovah with natural calamities. It was strictly a local judgment. "Blow ye the trumpet in Zion, and sound an alarm in my holy mountain; let all the inhabitants of the land tremble: For the day of Jehovah cometh, for it is nigh at hand; a day of darkness and gloominess, a day of clouds and thick darkness as the dawn spread upon the mountains . . ." (2:1-2). Of Judah's enemies, the prophet also said that "the earth quaketh before them, the heavens tremble; the sun and the moon are darkened, and the stars withdraw their shining" (2:10; see also 3:15). God used the heathen nation of Babylon to punish wayward Judah in 586 B.C. Indeed, when "Jehovah will roar from Zion . . . the heavens and the earth shall shake" (3:16).

In reproving the unfaithfulness of the people of Israel after their return from Babylonian captivity, Haggai promised that God would "shake the heavens and the earth and the sea and the dry land; [He] will shake all nations" (2:6-7). Verse 21 clearly shows that it is a temporal judgment of a local situation, yet the prophet used imagery drawn from greater natural phenomena as an exhortation to obedience.

Amos figuratively tells of the northern kingdom's ripeness for divine judgment, denoting the passing of an era: "I will cause the sun to go down at noon, and I will darken the earth on the clear day" (8:9). Thus, Samaria would soon fall. The same thing happened to Jerusalem in 586 B.C.: "Her sun is gone down while it was yet day" (Jer. 15:9; comp. with Isa. 60:20-21). Rather than continuing to bask in glory, Judah would suddenly perish. See also Isaiah 24:23 and 50:3.

Prophesying the end of ancient Egypt by Babylon, Ezekiel employed symbolism similar to Matthew 24:29. The prophet said that God would clothe heaven with blackness: "And when I shall extinguish thee [Egypt v. 2], I will cover the heavens, and make the moon stars thereof dark; I will cover the sun with a cloud and the moon shall not give its light" (32:7). These words described the end of an era and the establishment of another; it is impossible to apply Ezekiel's statement to the future end time.

Similarly, the *Testament of Moses,* dated early in the first century, describes the triumph over Israel's enemies: "And the earth will tremble, even to its ends shall it be shaken. And the high mountains will be made low. . . . The sun will not give light. And in darkness the horns of the moon will flee. Yea, they will be broken in pieces. It will be turned wholly into blood. Yea, even the circle of the stars will be thrown into disarray" (10:4-5). See also *II Baruch* 10:12.

Daniel's powerful "little horn" (8:9-10), thought by most scholars to be Antiochus Epiphanes, was an individual who could "cast stars down to the ground and trample upon them." A powerful and arrogant ruler is meting judgment upon the Jews. Through use of celestial imagery, Daniel prophetically described the fate of the noblemen of Israel in 165 B.C.,—its judges, leaders, priests, scribes and elders.

Therefore, in the passage under discussion, Matthew 24:29, Jesus, through use of heavenly elements, figuratively portrays the fall in AD 70 of Jerusalem's great political and religious nobility by employment of familiar and comprehensible Oriental images used by the prophets. These high, swelling terms emphasize the sad and troubled times amid the judgment of a decadent commonwealth. In early Jewish literature a shaking of the earth denoted political upheaval (*IV Ezra* 3:18, *I Maccabees* 1:28, *etc.*).

In Matthew 24:29, the "powers of heaven" were likely the leaders of mid-first century institutional Jewish religious groups, especially the seventy members of the Sanhedrin and other Jewish noblemen being removed from their high positions of judicial and ecclesiastical authority. The darkening sun and moon and the falling stars from heaven, a great picture of a collapsing universe, point to supernatural intervention into the affairs of Judea prior to its end in AD 70. Attempting to identify the precise meaning of the sun, the moon and the stars is not essential to an understanding of Matthew 24:29, anymore than analyzing each rainbow segment, the token of God's covenant with Noah, is necessary to determining the value of the colorful sign set in that ancient sky in Genesis 9.

The language of Matthew 24:29 coincides nearly verbatim with that used by Joel (2:30-31), when he prophesied the outpouring of the Holy Spirit, fulfilled on Pentecost (see Acts 2:19-20). Joel declared that the "sun shall be turned into darkness, and the moon into blood, before the great and terrible day of Jehovah cometh." On the Pentecost of Acts 2, Peter quoted this and other relevant parts of Joel and plainly declared a specific fulfillment: "this is that" (Acts 2:16), or amplified, "this is the beginning of that . . ."

As noted previously, the last part of this prophecy climaxing with the "day of the Lord," by the interpretive principle of correspondence must be properly applied to the same era, certainly within a generation. Fulfillment is therefore in the fall of Jerusalem. Bad exegesis and confusion result from overlooking this obvious early fulfillment in AD 70, and applying Joel's passage far into the future to the Lord's final coming at the end time.

Taking the "second coming" view, the millennial groups insist on a literal fulfillment of Matthew 24:29, a physical coming of the Christ in glory. Besides ignoring well established use of figurative language, such a view encounters other immense difficulties. While a darkening of the sun would also make the moon obscure, it is hardly conceivable that even one star could fall upon the earth, since all of them are much larger than this planet! And, most certainly, the massive moon could not defy physical law and turn into liquid blood, as Joel had literally stated. The passage therefore cannot be interpreted in the sense of obscuration or earthly destruction.

Late in the first century the author of *II Ezra* reacted to the destruction of the temple by worldly powers through the use of apocalyptic language: "And the sun shall suddenly shine forth at night, and the moon during the day. Blood shall drip from wood, and the stone shall utter its voice; the people shall be troubled, and the stars shall fall" (5:4-5). The writer foresaw the fall of the "land" then currently ruling, the Romans. See also 7:39.

The corresponding thought of Matthew 24:29 is in Luke 21:25-26, noticeable because of its different forms of expression. The latter simply mentions that "there shall be signs in sun and moon and stars." Luke, however, significantly adds, "and upon the earth [land, i.e., Judah] distress of nations, in perplexity for the roaring of the sea and the billows; men fainting from fear and for expectation of those things which are coming on the world: for the powers of the heavens shall be shaken." Luke is describing the wrath being poured out upon the entire nation of Israel in AD 70. See also the graphic description by Eusebius (*Eccl. Hist.* 2.26.1-3).

Luke's imagery of terrible calamity and great tumult and affliction among the people is shown by the roaring sea in agitation. The "perplexity" denotes their doubt and anxiety— uncertainty because of fear. The sea is an oft-used Jewish symbol of disturbed nations and society in restless upheaval. Earthly governments rose from the sea. Jeremiah reported that the nations were like mighty waters (46:7-10); when there was sorrow on the sea there was sorrow in society (49:23-24).

Isaiah said that the nations roared like the sea and flowed like the rushing of many waters: "Woe to the multitudes of many people, which make a noise like the noise of the seas; and to the rushing of nations, that make a noise like the noise of the seas; and to the rushing of nations, that make a rushing like the rushing of mighty waters" (17:12-13). That same prophet further declared that the wicked were like the troubled sea, restless (57:20). Daniel also wrote that mankind is a great sea of society (7:2-3, 17). Luke's tossing sea, then, embraces the anguished Jewish community, which was in tribulation and in a constant state of flux during the time just before its fall in the year 70. Thus, all of these celestial symbols denote impending judgment upon Jews contemporary with Christ, not something far into the future, at the end time.

On Clouds of Glory

Verse 30 of Matthew 24 furnishes additional symbols of judgment, with motifs and scriptural language again drawn from Old Testament material: "And then shall appear the sign of the Son of man in heaven; and then shall all the tribes of the earth [land] mourn, and they shall see the Son of man coming on the clouds of heaven with power and great glory." The text of Mark is substantially the same: "And then shall they see the Son of man coming in the clouds with great power and glory." *I Enoch* states that the Messiah (the elect one) would sit on the throne of glory (45:3, 51:3, 55:4, etc.).

Many people would apply this verse to the future "second coming" of Christ because it describes Him as "coming on the clouds." Premillennialists say that they are literal clouds lighted by His glory. But the Jewish prophet's use of the word "clouds" shows that "coming on the clouds" is also a figurative expression, a manifestation of the power of Yahweh.

Ezekiel plainly teaches that a time of clouds signifies judgment upon the nations: "For the day is near, even the day of Jehovah is near; it shall be a day of clouds, a time of the nations. And a sword shall come upon Egypt, and anguish shall be in Ethiopia, when the slain shall fall in Egypt; and they shall take away her multitude, and her foundations shall be broken down" (30:3-4). Concerning Egypt, Isaiah said that "Jehovah rideth upon a swift cloud and cometh unto Egypt" (19:1). All recognize that God did not literally appear visibly in the sky to the ancient Egyptians, while visiting that idolatrous nation in judgment.

Jeremiah declared that God shall come up as clouds on Judah (4:13). These were clouds of destruction. Similarly, as Jesus came upon the clouds against ungodly Jews, He would not physically be present in Jerusalem in AD 70, but would come in judgment through the power of the Roman military. His "presence" would be so real that all would recognize His influence in the destruction of the city, as though they had seen Him with their own eyes.

Several other Old Testament passages associate God with clouds. In Exodus 13:22 Jehovah went before the people by day in a pillar of a cloud. He thus descended upon Mt. Sinai, at the deliverance of the law (Exod. 34:5). He appeared in a cloud upon the mercy seat after Aaron's sons died (Lev. 16:2). In the temple the glory of Jehovah was in a cloud (I Kgs. 8:10-11); clouds are round about Him (Psa. 97:2). Another psalmist declared that God makes the clouds his chariot, showing his greatness (104:3). Specific association is also in Psalm 18:10-12: "At the brightness before him His thick clouds passed." In Ezekiel's description of a vision of Jehovah (1:4-14), a great cloud contained God's four living creatures. See also Daniel 7:13-14, Exodus 16:10, (19:9), Numbers 11:25, Joel 2:1-2, Nahum 1:3, and Zephaniah 1:14-15.

And so, to describe the destruction of Jerusalem in AD 70 by the Romans, Jesus used long-established apocalyptic language. But the Lord did not have to appear bodily and physically in order to "come" upon the apostate nation, anymore than did God in ancient times appeared to Israel corporally and in a human-recognized form (Ex., 3:8, Psa. 72:6, Gen. 11:5; see also Zech. 2:10-11).

Matthew 24:30 also mentions the "sign of the Son of man in heaven." At Matthew 24:3 the disciples asked, "What will be the sign of thy coming?" Previous comment on that verse shows that any "second coming" is impossible because at that time the disciples did not believe He would be killed! The coming is literally "presence." Therefore, the sign of verse 30 denotes nothing veiled or mysterious, such as a mystical heavenly cross, a star, a lightning flash, or a host of angels, but is merely figurative of Christ's presence in judgment against "the heavens'"— the Jewish societies and corrupt religious leadership.

The verse also mentions that "all of the tribes of the earth [land] shall mourn." Zechariah confines a similarly worded passage to Israel only, nothing universal, in saying, "In that day shall there be a great morning in Jerusalem. . .and the land shall mourn, every family apart. . . ." (12:10-12). The localized events of Micah 1:2-7 show the Lord going forth from the sanctuary to punish the crimes of Samaria and Judah, yet all of the earth is described as affected: "Hear ye peoples, all of you; hearken, O earth, and that thereon is. . ." (v. 2). Haggai said that God would shake "all nations and the precious things of all nations," yet the people of Judah alone are being reproved (2:6-7). The apparent worldwide punishment of Isaiah 13:6-11 is a burden only on a solitary locality—Babylon (v. 1).

It is therefore not uncommon to couch local oracles of judgment in universal and radical language. The mourning of all the tribes likely refers to the lamentations of Jewish families living not only in Judea but also scattered throughout the Roman Empire, grieved because of the destruction of the temple and the terrible loss of kinsmen. The sorrow to come upon all tribes of the land, and not the nations of the earth, is therefore coincident with the desolation of Zion, the Jewish dominion, instead of events in a distant age. The millennial reference to evildoers who pierced Jesus in every age since the time of Christ is not suggested by the text.

After mention of the Son of man coming in a cloud with power and great glory, Luke adds an additional thought at this point in the narrative: "But when these things begin to come to pass, look up, and lift up your heads; because your redemption draweth nigh" (21:28). Jesus' disciples were to recognize "these things" and then they could raise their heads in exultant expectation of their speedy redemption, a deliverance not from sin (something they already possessed because of their covenant relationship with God), or their bodies in the resurrection, but a release from persecuting Jews in Jerusalem in the late AD 60s. The Son of man would come in power and glory in the Roman armies to destroy Jerusalem, the seat of obstinate, Talmudic fanaticism.

Matthew 24:31: Trumpets ... Angels ... Winds

Verse 31 continues the thought of the preceding two verses: "And He shall send forth His angels with a great sound of a trumpet." Far from speaking of a yet future reign of saints into heaven, these words announce that Christ shall send forth among the nations gospel messengers who proclaim the message of salvation, calling people to obedience. After Jerusalem fell and the people of Christ in all quarters were unshackled from fanatical Judaism, the gospel would multiply and ultimately successfully sweep the empire (see Acts 17:6), a firm reality by the early third century. Orthodox Judaism would be thrust out, as in Luke 13:28-29, and instead people from every compass point would sit down in God's kingdom. Thus, instead of assembling annually at Jerusalem in the temple, God's scattered chosen ones would forever unite around the triumphant Son of man.

In Old Testament times a trumpet sound might call attention to many things (Judg. 7:19-22, Ezek. 7:14), especially in calling together the assembly "at the door of the tabernacle of the congregation" (Num. 10:3). Now, in Matthew 24:31, with the sounding trumpet, Jesus gathers together all persevering believers, the remnant to be spared from the destruction throughout Judea. This dramatic divine rescue operation, as part of the *parousia* of Christ, did not take place just once in AD 70 but potentially could occur over and over in history, in that the gospel still gathers elect souls unto Christ to build His *ekklesia* from all quarters of the political heaven (see Milton Terry, *Biblical Hermeneutics,* p. 447n).

The angels would "gather the elect from the four winds, from one end of the heaven to the other" (v. 31b). Mark reads,". . .from the uttermost part of the earth to the uttermost part of heaven. . ." (13:27; see also Deut. 30:4; Zech. 2:6). Far from being a literal description, or depiction of a scene visible to human eyes, this phrase figuratively tells how the preaching of the Christ would regain chosen people who had gone astray. Faithful Jews would be gathered out of all lands and established forever upon the spiritual mountain of God (Amos 9:14-15; Jer. 23:5-8, 32:37-44; Ezek. 37:21-22).

Gathering scattered people was a function attributable to God in days of old, for He said, "I will gather them from the countries, and will bring them into their own land" (Ezek. 34:13; see also 36:24, Deut. 30:3-4; Isa. 43:5-6). God could scatter His people (Zech. 2:6), as well as gather them (Psa. 50:3-5), returning His people from Babylon to the land of Judah in one day (Isa. 66:8-9).

The Greek *aggeleos,* translated either angels or messengers, refers to John the Baptist (Mark 1:2), angels near Jesus' tomb (Luke 24:23), disciples of Jesus (Luke 9:52), a "messenger of Satan" (II Cor 12:7), and even to Joshua's spies (Jas. 2:25), as well as the angels in the more commonly understood sense of heavenly beings and ministering spirits who intervene in earthly events, as those who assisted Christ after His temptation and at His resurrection (Matt. 4:11, 28:2). An angel spoke to Moses in the burning bush (Acts 7:30, 38); others directed Philip (Acts 8:26), Cornelius (Acts 10:3-7), and Paul (Acts 27:23-24). The "angels" of Matthew 24:31 (Mark 8:38, 13:27) may well refer to the apostles and disciples who were sent forth into all of the first century world to preach Christ's gospel.

The four winds in Jewish writings metaphorically denote the wide extent of the earth, as in Jeremiah 49:36: "And upon

Elam I will bring the four winds from the four quarters of heaven," and in Zechariah 2:6, ". . . I have spread you abroad as the four winds of the heavens." In Daniel 7:2 the four winds of heaven break forth upon the great sea of society, from whence come the nations (vv. 3-8; (see also Ezek. 37:9, Rev. 7:1, *II Esdras 13:5*; comp. Luke 13:29). The last part of verse 30 "from one end of heaven to the other," means that people from all economic classes in the Roman Empire would respond affirmatively to the gospel, as described above.

Verses 32-33 relate a parable derived from a budding fig tree, inviting a comparison with the events of the previous verses. They state, "When his branch is yet tender, and putteth forth leaves, ye know that summer is nigh: so likewise ye, when ye shall see all these things, know that it is near, even at the doors." According to the parallel passage, Luke 21:31, the "it" is the kingdom of God. The comparison is not apparent until it is determined what is meant by "all these things" in verse 33, a phrase which is repeated in the very next verse: "This generation shall not pass till *all these things* be accomplished." When identical expressions appear in consecutive sentences, they must refer to the same thing, unless between them the author might introduce something striking to force a different meaning on the second occurrence. In the first part of verse 34 no new information exists to suggest a change of meaning.

Therefore, in the same way that the coming of summer is imminent when the fig tree covers itself with leaves, the disciples could know that Jerusalem's destruction was at hand, when they would see all these things, namely, the signs of the false christs, earthquakes, wars in various places, the abomination of desolation, etc. (Matt. 24:5-15). It would be time to flee the city (vv. 16-19).

Summary

The darkening of the sun and moon, the falling of the stars, and the shaking of the powers of the heavens, is language borrowed from ancient hieroglyphics, where such symbols represented the fall of ancient states and nobility. It is not language which demands literal or natural fulfillment. These apocalyptical forms of speech are part and parcel of the genius of the prophetic Hebrew scriptures.

In Matthew 24:29 these convulsions of heavenly bodies denote the extinction of the prosperity and privilege of the Jewish nation and the overthrow of Talmudic Judaism. The disturbances of the sun, moon, and stars would be evident signs of divine interference in the affairs of Judea late in the decade of 60, showing that the Son of man was indeed reigning from heaven (a rule that began soon after His resurrection), from whence He came in AD 70, riding upon the clouds of heaven in power and great glory in judgment against godless people who would not allow Him to reign over them (Luke 19:14).

The counsels and admonitions embodied in the heavenly figurative language of verses 29 and 30 were clearly addressed to first century disciples; people of subsequent generations would not see the signs which legitimately had been fulfilled in the destruction of Jerusalem. By its yet future application of these symbolic figures to events far from the time of the fall of Judea in AD 70, millennial sectarians of all kinds fail to do justice to the words of Christ concerning His coming on clouds amid the decline of sun, moon, and stars against godless people.

GARDEN OF GETHSEMANE   A STREET IN JERUSALEM

Chapter Twelve

'THIS GENERATION
SHALL NOT PASS...'

THROUGHOUT THE FIRST 33 verses of Matthew 24, Jesus told His awestruck disciples about the destruction of the magnificent temple and of the city which had murdered the prophets (23:34-36). He emphatically remarked concerning the longstanding temple that the day would come in which "there shall not be left here one stone upon another, that shall not be thrown down" (24:2).

In response to the Master's startling announcement of the temple's demise, the disciples asked privately, "Tell us, when shall these things be? and what shall be the sign of thy coming [parousia]?" The presence of Christ would take place after a series of events and signs consisting of the appearance of false teachers, rumors of wars, apostasy, the abomination of desolation, tribulation, and several other incidents.

In all of these things, there is no hint that any of these things would take place in conjunction with a Jewish generation at a yet-future time—that the coming of Christ would be separated by a vast time period. Rather, from Jesus' announcement throughout Matthew 24 the temple's demise and the signs preceding it would occur *immediately* (v. 29). Some of the inquisitive disciples of verse four (see also Mark 9:1) would live to experience everything in their generation. Therefore, Jesus admonished His followers that "when ye see all these things, know ye that he is near, even at the doors" (v.33).

The Generation of "All These Things"

The key passage Matthew 24:33-34 determines the time element. It solemnly declares that "Verily I say unto you, *this* generation shall not pass away till all these things be accomplished." The NEB translates this verse, "I tell you this: the present generation will live to see it all," a rendering nearly the same as the Moffatt Translation. Today's English Version reads, "Remember this! All these things will happen before the people now living have all died." Therefore, "all these things" of necessity embraces all signs and events outlined in Matthew 24:3-33.

Nevertheless, what "all these things" means is a point of serious dispute with various millennial groups, who would assign the generation of verse 34 to the last one at the future end time. Such an application could hardly be true, in view of the linguistic structure of Jesus' Olivet discourse in Matthew 24, Mark 13, and Luke 21. Note the repetition of the key phrase "these things" in the discourse at 24:2, 3, 5, and 8. Luke, in verses 21:28, 31, and 32, uses this phrase in connection with the highly figurative and controversial sun, moon, and stars (compare with Matthew 24:29). See also Luke 21:6, 7, 9, 12, and especially verse 36.

Daniel 12:7 employs the phrase "all these things" in a context which prophesies of the "abomination of desolation" which Jesus in Matthew 24:15 definitely ascribes to the time before the destruction of Jerusalem. Therefore, the structure of Matthew 24 and Luke 21 binds "all these things" to *all* events mentioned in the discourse. The fulfillment emphatically took place before the generation of Jews to whom Jesus was speaking had passed away.

Jesus had in mind only the then-current generation because He used the very same phrase earlier in the day to pronounce woes on the tradition-steeped Pharisees, concluding with, "Verily, I say unto you, all these things shall come upon this generation (Matt. 23:36). Considering the repetition of the key phrase and the context, the only defensible conclusion is that the disciples contemporary with Christ would witness the fulfillment of His prophetic word, culminating with the fall of Jerusalem and the dismantling of the temple late in the summer of the year 70.

Matthew's gospel thoroughly describes this generation of orthodox Jews in Jesus' time. Its party leaders were faithless and perverse (17:17), unrepentant, evil and sign-seeking (16:3-4), ill-tempered and capricious (11:16-19), wicked and very adulterous (12:39), evil-speaking, inhuman (23:4, 14), tradition-steeped (15:9), and sinful. That generation was destined for condemnation (12:41-42), for it had rejected the Christ (Luke 17:25). It was worse than previous generations (Matt. 12:45). In fact, Jesus promised to heap upon it the blood of prophets from Abel to Zechariah (23:35).

The hypocritical Pharisees of that generation had shut up the kingdom of God against others (Matt. 23:13); and the lawyers had taken away the key of knowledge (Luke 11:52). It was the generation from which Peter admonished others to save themselves (Acts 2:40), because the nation's disaster course would be realized in AD 70.

That the generation of verse 34 is Christ's is also borne out by scholarship. The Greek word for generation is *genea*, meaning "an age or progeny. . . It does not denote a period of unlimited duration." Thus, generation does not mean off-spring, nation, or stock. Parallel renditions of generation are "brood" and "progeny," as in "generation of vipers" / "brood of vipers" (see Matt. 3:7, 12:34, etc.).

All understand "brood" as progeny hatched at one time.

W.E. Vine says that *genea* means "a whole multitude of men (a progeny) living at the same time, especially those of the Jewish race" (*Dictionary of New Testament Words*, p. 44). Examples of such usage are Luke 1:50, 11:50-51; Acts 13:36; Hebrews 3:10. When Jesus spoke of generation, He always referred to his contemporaries, as in the citations above from the gospel of Matthew.

Others insist that the word "generation" means "race." *Genea is* used in this sense sparingly in the "New Testament," for example at I Peter 2:9: "But ye are an elect race, a royal priesthood, a holy nation." But if generation means "race" in Matthew 24:34, then Jesus erred in logic. After enumerating certain events affecting the Jews (vv. 5-33), He would have uttered a simplistic truism in verse 34, if He said that the Jewish race would not pass away until all things that would happen to the Jewish race would happen to it! Therefore, the word "generation" conveys its ordinary meaning. Millennialists who insist upon defining generation as "race" in the book of Matthew can count only to one! (see Matt. 1:17).

Modern Israel – Fulfillment of Prophecy?

Most millennialists say that the birth of ethnic Israel as a nation in 1947 in Palestine is a strong indicator that the world is in the time of the latter days. In *The Late Great Planet Earth,* Hal Lindsey sees this reestablishment as the fig tree of Matthew 24:33 sprouting its first leaves. The signs of the times of Matthew 24 would all be displayed before the generation ends, usually defined as a forty year period.

But the clock ran out on Lindsey years ago, in that the generation of 1948-1988 passed with no fulfillment of the elements of Jesus' Olivet discourse, such as the abomination of desolation and the coming of the Son of man, among others.

Since this explanation of end times failed, Lindsey then

tried to make "this generation" refer to an indefinite "terminal generation" before the "second coming" of Christ. But no one can know with certainty when such a time period actually would begin. In explaining "this generation shall not pass away. . ." Lindsey also said, "As long as one person who was alive in 1948 is still living, the clock has not run out."

In contrast with such speculation, the first century disciples of Christ did see *every* event mentioned in the Olivet discourse come to pass before Jerusalem's demise in AD 70. Nothing Jesus said indicated that fulfillment would have to await the establishment of the modern state of Israel.

As ably pointed out by John Bray, twentieth century Israel is not contemplated in Matthew 24 because, contrary to popular premillennial views, there is no such thing as a "Jewish race," because of mixed blood lines through centuries of interracial marriages. In fact, the modern Jew has no physical connection with the biblical Jew. Today's Jews have as ancestors the Khazars of the Black Sea area, which as a nation in about AD 740 adopted the Jewish religion. Therefore, there is a considerable difference between a first century *Israelite* and a twentieth-century *Israeli.*

Various popular encyclopaedias and even the *Encyclopaedia Judaica* admit that the Jews of today do not constitute a distinct race. Wherever Jews have lived for generations, their physical traits have come to approximate those of indigenous people. Jews, therefore, have no uniform characteristics, whether physically, ornamentally or philosophically. Instead, the worldwide common tie is some form of Judaistic religion.

The main part of twentieth-century Jewry therefore never originated in Palestine. Even the focal point of the ancient nation of Israel was not race, but the fact that as Abraham's descendents the people enjoyed a covenant with the gracious One who had led them out of Egypt. God's choice to interdwell with a people was never made on the basis of race or blood but rather on covenant, in a relationship with true believers.

Therefore, the establishment of the state of Israel in 1947 is not a biblical fulfillment in prelude to a restoration of the Jews, together with a rebuilt temple with sacrifices offered in it. Such a theory is not even in accord with classical premillennial views of some early church fathers, for Papias, Tertullian, and others of the second and third centuries did not believe in a literal restoration of territory for the Jews or a re-establishment of ancient temple rituals.

The Passing of Heaven and Earth

Matthew 24:35, "Heaven and earth shall pass away, but my words shall not pass away," also denotes the ongoing process of judgment which was taking place against the wayward nation. Several biblical references show that the phrase "heaven and earth" is a figurative expression to denote the Jewish economy, its religious society and government. Moses used the term "heaven and earth" as an attention getter to represent the Jewish economy in Deuteronomy 32:1: "Give ear, ye heavens, and I will speak; And let the earth hear the words of my mouth."

Similar usages are by Isaiah in 1:2, 34:1, 49:13, 51:6, 66:22, and by Haggai in 2:6, 21. Psalm 102:25-27 employs the phrase "heaven and earth" to contrast the enduring qualities of God's word with the temporality of things in the created universe. In *IV Ezra* 3:18, written about AD 100, God "didst bend down the heavens and shake the earth and move the world" in describing the Lord's leading His people out of Egypt to Mount Sinai. Still another author used that phrase to tell of the end of one world and the expectation of a new order (II Peter 3:13). In all instances, one system is taking the place of another, as explained earlier commenting on Isaiah 65 and 66 and Joel 3:14-17.

Luke 16:17 declares that "it is easier for heaven and earth to pass away than for one tittle of the law to fall." Again, the Jewish society is meant. In the Sermon on the Mount (Matt. 5:18), Jesus declared, "Till heaven and earth pass away, one jot or one tittle shall in no wise pass away till all things be accomplished." All things needed to be fulfilled which had been written in the Psalms, Moses, and in the scrolls of the other prophets (Luke 24:44; see also John 17:4). The last of these temporal events would be the dissolution of the Jewish economy in AD 70.

Matthew 24:36 states that no one would know the day or hour, hence Jesus' admonition to His disciples of that generation to watch and be ready (vv. 42, 44). The day would be a time period of inconvenience to nursing mothers (Matt. 24:19) and of great tribulation which would destroy much flesh (vv. 21-22). The day therefore could not refer to the yet future judgment after the final return of the Christ, who would certainly know when He would return after being restored to glory with the Father. Jesus possesses "all the treasure of wisdom and knowledge hidden" (Col. 2:3).

The days of the coming of the Son of man would come as unexpectedly upon Judea as the arrival of flood waters upon the wicked community of Noah (Gen. 6:5; 7:6-24). People were going about their lives, eating and drinking, marrying and giving in marriage, until they were surprised by the rising waters, despite the frequent warnings and admonitions given by Noah, the preacher of righteousness.

Now in the first century, Jesus said that the tribulation upon Jerusalem would develop when people would be engaged in ordinary day-to-day business and common pleasures, little expecting the ruin of their economy until trouble was upon them. But heeders of Christ's warnings, as expressed in Matthew 24:5-33, would be rescued from the destruction of the city, even as Lot was saved from the burning of Sodom (Luke 17:28-32) and Noah from the antediluvian world. Similarly, the indifferent would be left to perish during the Roman invasion of Jerusalem in AD 70. Therefore, the Master urged

constant preparation (vv. 43-44) to escape calamity by recognizing the signs which would precede the fall of the nation.

After foretelling the end of the nation and His coming
through the Roman armies in His messianic reign, Jesus also
looked further beyond to the ultimate fate of all individuals, as
expressed by the word "then" in Matthew 25:1 (see also. v.
31). Matthew 25 records three impressive parables that ad-
monish His disciples to be active in the kingdom, urging
watchfulness and readiness. The series culminates in the powerful, sublime scene of the future general last judgment of all
people (vv. 31-46), an event that was presaged by His earlier
parousia, the coming in judgment against Jerusalem in AD 70.
In that case, the destruction of the city served as a type and
image of the universal judgment to come.

Chapter Thirteen

OTHER NEW TESTAMENT
REFERENCES TO AD 70

I N THE LAST WEEK OF HIS EARTHLY LIFE, Jesus made other references to wayward Israel's terrible fate in AD 70,
besides those recorded in Matthew 22 to 24. By night the be-
trayer Judas led a multitude of Jews, including some of their
leaders who were armed with swords and staves, to capture
Jesus (Matt. 26:47-49). In response to Peter's defense of the
Master, Jesus said, "Put up again thy sword into its place; for
all they that take the sword shall perish with the sword" (v.
52). Presenting a general principle that violent people often die
a similar type death, Jesus also may have been reminding His
disciples that the sword would be the instrument of the fanatical Jews' own destruction within their lifetimes.

During His trial before the Sanhedrin, Jesus was plainly
asked by Caiaphas the high priest if He were the Christ (Matt.
26:62-63). Answering affirmatively, Jesus also said, "Henceforth ye shall see the Son of man sitting at the right hand of
Power, and coming on the clouds of heaven" (v. 64). Mark
reads essentially the same (14:62) but Luke at this point reads

slightly differently: "From henceforth shall the Son of man be seated at the right hand of the power of God" (22:69).

To "see" means to recognize that in the events leading to the fall of Judea in AD 70, the Jewish nation would know that Jesus had a hand in it all. The "seeing" is not physical, but in the power and wrath of divine vengeance. Thus, in the course of his lifetime, the high priest as well as his associates would experience the divine judgment to be brought against the entire nation, especially the religious hierarchy. Jesus would figuratively come on clouds of judgment, in which His heavenly authority was manifested on earth through the Roman army.

On the occasion when Pilate washed his hands before a crowd of Jews, the people responded to that act by saying, "His blood be on us and on our children" (Matt. 27:25). Evidently these Jews accepted the blood guiltiness and the consequences for crucifying Jesus. The implication was fearfully answered by destruction in AD 70. The Jews also had to answer for the righteous blood of generations of prophets (Matt. 23:35). In committing the national crime of murder, they would pay a national penalty—death; the blood of Christ then would be expiated by the blood of the people.

While Jesus was on his way to His cross, a great number of people, including women, bewailed and lamented Him. In response to the crowd Christ said, "Daughters of Jerusalem, weep not for me, but weep for yourselves, and for your children. For behold, the days are coming, in which they shall say, 'Blessed are the barren, and the wombs that never bare, and the breasts that never gave suck' " (Luke 23:27-29). The broken-hearted Jesus knew well the woes coming upon them in the destruction of the city within their generation. Because of the distress of the tribulation, the blessed would indeed be the childless.

In verse 30 the Jews would cry for protection by appealing to the mountains and the hills: "Then shall they begin to say to the mountains, 'Fall on us;' and to the hills, 'Cover us.' " The mountains and the hills are synonymous through parallelism. This proverbial expression describes a future horrifying time in one locality, Judea, when persecuted people would desperately seek any shelter or refuge.

In similar situations, Jewish prophets recorded that people sought refuge among the rocks because of impending calamity. Men hid in caves in Isaiah's figurative description of the fall of Jerusalem in 586 B.C. (2:19, 21). In a judgment of Samaria, mentioned in Hosea 10:7-8, the people cried to the mountains to cover them during the destruction. Similarly, in Luke 23:30, the wrath of Christ in glory and in a local judgment would descend upon the city in the year 70. See also Revelation 6:16, wherein the same imagery refers to a still later time when people would beseech God to spare them from the wrath of His destruction, Christ's coming in judgment against the Roman Empire.

The thought concludes with the proverb in verse 31: "For if they do these things in a green tree, what shall be done in the dry?" In other words, if rebellious Jews would betray the Christ, the hope of the Jewish nation in a time of peace, what horrors awaited the nation itself? The green tree probably embraces the unlawful plot and crucifixion instigated by the Jewish leaders in the final week of Christ. The dry tree is decadent Jerusalem and its political and religious hierarchy before AD 70, ready to be consumed like a heap of dry wood.

The Epistles to the Thessalonians

Not long after Paul had preached in Thessalonica on his second missionary journey, he wrote them about the wrath which would be poured out to the uttermost (I Thess. 2:16). This wrath consists of a revelation of the Lord Jesus from heaven "taking vengeance" upon the disobedient and the willfully ignorant of God (Rom. 1:18-32) in a day wherein they would experience "flaming fire and the punishment of everlasting destruction and exclusion from the presence of the Lord" (II Thess. 1:7-8).

At first glance, these strong epithets might appear to refer to a temporal calamity occurring in perhaps just one nation, Judea, even as Isaiah described the distress to come upon Jerusalem in 586 B.C.: "The sinners in Zion are afraid: fearfulness hath surprised the hypocrites. Who among us shall dwell with the devouring fire? Who among us shall dwell with everlasting burnings?" (33:14).

But verses 7-8 in context is concerned with the "punishment of eternal destruction and exclusion from the presence of the Lord and from the glory of His might" (v. 9) — a general judgment, not a localized one. Significantly, the word *parousia,* a "coming" of Christ commonly associated with the judgment of Judea (as in Matthew 24), is *not* used in II Thessalonians 1:7-8. Instead, this judgment is a "revelation" from heaven of Jesus and His angels (v. 7), words which harmonize well with the yet future universal judgment of the people in all nations, as proclaimed by Jesus Himself in Matthew 25:31-46 (see also Rev. 20:11-15).

In *Against Heresies* III:27.1, Irenaeus properly associated II Thessalonians 1:7-9 with the condemnation of sinners and the end time judgment, even as Paul said to the Romans, "For the wrath of God shall be revealed from heaven against all ungodliness and unrighteousness of men who hold back the truth in unrighteousness (1:18).

Further, II Thessalonians 1 seems to complement Paul's discussion of the "coming of the Lord" in his first letter to them (4:13-5:11), where the apostle discusses the great assembly of the saints who will meet the Lord at the end time. That lengthy passage extensively treats the subject of the final return of Christ in prelude to the universal judgment. Everyone alive at that time will join all past saints to participate in the same blessing of a physical resurrection from the dead (I Thess. 4:14; see also I Cor. 15:12-34, II Cor. 4:14f). Such teaching is an integral part of the gospel of Christ.

The earliest church fathers are of one mind in affirming a future universal physical resurrection of the dead. In about AD 95, Clement of Rome urged his readers to believe that Christ would come again (*I Clement* Ch. 23). About forty years later, Polycarp said that God "who raised Him from the dead will raise us up also . . ." (*To the Philippians* 2:1). In his epistle to the Trallians in about AD 107, Ignatius echoed an identical hope (10:1). In *To Smyrna*, the bishop contended against contemporary Gnostics who would deny a bodily resurrection (Chs. 3, 7). Christ's physical resurrection is a proof of ours, according to Irenaeus in about AD 180 (*Against Heresies* II:19.6; see also IV:40:2 and V:3.3, 5.1-2, 15.1).

In mid-second century, Justin Martyr wrote an extensive treatise on the resurrection of the dead, arguing that since Christ was raised bodily, we will also (see also *Dialogue with Trypho,* Chs. 21, 49, 52, and 110-111). Furthermore, among the Jews the doctrine of a physical resurrection blossomed during the intertestamental period to become a prominent part of rabbinic thought by the time of Christ. This truth was on the lips of Martha while she talked to Jesus about the "last day" (John 11:24; see also 6:39-40).

And so, any ancient attempt by various heretical Gnostic sects to spiritualize the doctrine of the resurrection obviously encountered consistent united testimony of the above witnesses. Any modern sects, including Jehovah Witnesses and Seventh Day Adventists, who would spiritualize this doctrine, are not far from beliefs of the long-condemned Gnostics.

The Man of Sin

In II Thessalonians 2:1-10, the apostle Paul describes a "coming (*parousia*) of the Lord" (vv. 1, 8), a temporal judgment against Judea. Such teaching coincides nicely with the *parousia* of Christ in Matthew 24. But this "coming" before the end of the Jewish commonwealth would not occur "except there come a falling away first," and the revelation of the man of sin, the lawless one. This individual has been the touchstone of wild and unusual religious speculation. This lawless one would manifest himself during a time of apostasy (v. 3), which probably occurred very late in the decade of AD 60, and is more particularly described in the epistle to the Hebrews (6:6; 10:26, 39).

He "opposeth and exalteth himself above all that is called God or that is worshipped" (v. 4) and sat in God's temple (v. 4b). His iniquitous work was already underway when Paul wrote the epistle (v. 7). But Jesus would come—a spiritual presence (see v. 1)—and would slay this lawless one (v. 8).

This "man of sin" is not the late-first century antichrist, as embodied in Docetic and Gnostic sects (I John 2:18, 22; 4:3; II John 7). While the antichrist has broad application, recurring over and over in history, Paul's man of sin is definitely one person—likely a Jewish high priest at Jerusalem who presided in the temple sanctuary. He held office in the central temple building itself, as distinct from the accessory structures and courts. This sanctuary is the same as Matthew's "holy place" (24:15), wherein the abomination of desolation resided. As concluded earlier, this "desolating sacrilege" was a man, probably the unrighteous high priest Phanni. Apparently the "man of sin" is the same individual.

There are earlier precedents in the Jewish writings which describe certain office holders as "gods." Isaiah describes a man in a high place at Babylon who exalted himself as god (14:4, 12-14, 22). He was the haughty King Nebuchadnezzar, who would be cast down from the political heaven, for God would rise up against him. Ezekiel describes the Prince of Tyre as rich, wanting nothing (28:2, 6, 11-12). "I am a god," he said, but Yahweh would bring him down, humble him. Belshazzar also exalted himself high above the Lord (Dan. 5:23), but his kingdom was found wanting by the true God, and his empire was felled in a single night. Psalm 82:6-7 describes certain office holders as "gods."

Defining the identity of Paul's man of sin is admittedly difficult. Perhaps his true identity may never be determined.

The Epistle to the Hebrews

In view of the troubled times before the fall of Jerusalem, the author of the letter to the Hebrews warned his readers not to abandon the faith in time of danger. He urged them not to cast away their courage and confidence (3:14, 4:16, 10:19), for faith even now has great recompense of reward (10:22, 39). He further admonished them "to provoke unto love and good works; not forsaking our own assembling together . . . but exhorting one another; and so much the more, as ye see the day draweth nigh" (10:24-25).

This "day" of tribulation and judgment was one which by spiritual discernment the saints in Judea could plainly perceive approaching. The continual refusal of the obstinate, rebellious Jewish nation to turn to Christ and repent of spiritual wickedness clearly presaged the bursting forth of God's wrath against them. As tribulation upon Jerusalem and finally its destruction approached, the flames of apostasy were dampened as saints comforted and exhorted one another in the assemblies and in occasional meetings.

A reference to the first day of the week as the "day" of Hebrews 10:25 is not reasonable. Are we, for instance, told to exhort brethren more on Friday than on Thursday, and more on Saturday than Friday? There is even less justification for applying the "day" to the end time judgment, something that even now we cannot see approaching, much less could the saints in the first century.

Knowing in advance that Christ would visit Jerusalem in judgment in their time was thus an incentive to fidelity. The basis for exhorting was Jesus' words as recorded in Matthew 24, as well as many other gospel admonitions and warnings uttered by Jesus, which related to the passing of the nation.

In Hebrews 10:37, the author demonstrated the certainty of the enemy coming upon Jerusalem. "He that cometh shall come, and shall not tarry," refers back to Habakkuk 2:3, wherein the prophet foretold the swiftness of Nebuchadnezzar's first coming upon Jerusalem in 606 B.C. The prophet was making preparations for the judgment which would mean the close of Judah's early history, with the end coming at the fall of Jerusalem to the Chaldeans in 586 B.C.

The author of Hebrews made the same application, except that the enemy was Rome and the time was the year 70. Judea would be subdued and party-ridden Judaism would be dealt a severe blow. The beginning of the verse reads, "For yet a very little while . . ." The literal reading is "a very, very little while." The Roman conquest of Jerusalem took place just a few years after the letter to the Hebrews was sent to its recipients.

Throughout the Hebrew letter the author explains that Christ is the better way—superior to angels, Moses, the familiar priesthood of Aaron, and in Jesus' mediatorship, priesthood, and sacrifice. Jesus' blood sacrifice to validate the eternal covenant (Heb. 13:20) renders the Mosaic animal sacrifices obsolete. Thus at 8:13 the author explains, "But that which is becoming old and waxeth aged is nigh unto vanishing away," Redemption through Christ began after the cross, in AD 33. By the time of the writing of Hebrews, AD 65–67, longstanding Jewish concepts were "nigh unto vanishing away" to be eliminated completely in only a few short years when the great temple in Jerusalem would be destroyed, along with obsolete animal sacrifices, genealogies, and the Levitical priesthood, as well as all other non-moral aspects of Moses' law.

Hebrews 12:26-28 contrasts things moveable with the immovable. ". . . [God] whose voice then shook the earth: but now He hath promised, saying, 'Yet once more will I make to tremble not the earth only, but also the heaven.' And this word, 'Yet once more' signifieth the removing of those things that are shaken . . . That these things which are not shaken may remain. Wherefore, receiving a kingdom that cannot be shaken . . . "

The expression, "Yet once more . . . " implies that there will be a shaking that will dwarf other similar judgments. It is a quotation from Haggai 2:6, where the prophet described a new order of things. The shaking of the heaven and the earth is, as previously noted, a figurative description of great political and social change. The "removing of things that are shaken" is the destruction of the Jewish order by Rome. In verse 28, Christ's kingdom, or kingship, which cannot be shaken, is compared with the Jewish kingdom which is about to be shaken.

Hebrews 13:12 tells of Jesus suffering outside of the city gates of Jerusalem; the next verse declares that messianic Jews must religiously separate themselves from degenerate Jerusalem—by going beyond it because, as the next verse states, "we have not here an abiding city." Destruction came in AD 70. Instead, the saints of God were admonished to look eagerly for the eternal city to come—heaven (v. 14). Finally, in the midst of the Jewish revolt, the author describes God as the "God of peace" (13:20; see also Ezek. 37:26). Truly, the end of all things of institutional Judaism was near.

James and Peter

James, who probably wrote in the decade of 60, warned his readers of the folly of heaping treasures together in the "last days" (5:3; compare with the phrase "at the end of these days" in Heb. 1:2). This is the time when the coming national judgment on Judea was close at hand. The author admonishes his Jewish readers (v. 1:1) to be patient "until the coming of the Lord" (5:7). The coming is, literally, "presence," and in AD 68-70 it would bring relief to the suffering Jewish faithful from fanatical kinsmen on every hand. The "Judge standing before the doors" (5:9) indicates the nearness of Christ coming in judgment; His instrument was the might of the Roman armies.

In his first epistle, Peter wrote that the end of all things was at hand, indicating perhaps that the fall of Jerusalem was not far off (4:7). But the fiery trial (vv. 12-14) is a separate event which will occur at the *revelation* of His glory (v. 13), and thus it is not a *parousia* or coming of Christ upon ungodly Jews. Instead, the suffering is social and political, for the author speaks well of kings and governors, the ruling authorities of the Roman Empire (2:15f). Verse 17 is also not a localized judgment but a universal one (comp. with II Thess. 1:7-8).

The Book of Revelation

John's Apocalypse stands in the mainline of prophetic tradition. Chapters 6 through 19 are an unveiling of future events "shortly to come to pass" after the apostle John had written the book of Revelation toward the end of the reign of the Roman Emperor Domitian in about AD 95, a time of writing faithfully preserved in oral tradition and reported by Irenaeus in about the year 180, as well as by several other church fathers over the next 350 years.

In Revelation 12:1-17, the story flow is abruptly halted by the introduction of a celestial figure, as recorded by John: "And a great sign was seen in heaven: a woman arrayed with the sun, and the moon under her feet, and upon her head a crown of twelve stars" (v.1). This imagery appears to be a flashback to events much earlier than those developing at the close of the first century, the time and setting for the events of John's visions.

Embodied in this woman in travail (v. 2) are centuries of people of the faithful covenant remnant of Israel (the Old Testament *ekklesia*) ardently longing for the Christ, the manchild of verse five. Jeremiah characterized Israel as a woman (2:32), as did Isaiah (50:1, 54:1-3, 66:7) and Hosea (2:2-7).

The great and dreadful fiery-red dragon, (v. 3), destructive and corruptive in purpose, was bent upon murdering the manchild at his birth. Failing in that (v. 5), he relentlessly pursued the woman on earth (v. 13). But God had given the woman wings to escape from the dragon (vv. 14; see also v. 6).

Thus, verses 6 and 14-16 might well describe the fortunes of the woman who by then had passed from symbolizing the longstanding Jewish covenant remnant into the expanded form of God's people under Christ, including messianic Jews residing in Jerusalem during the tribulation and wars of AD 66-70.

During that time there was a gradual withdrawal of the faithful from Jerusalem, fleeing into the mountain wilderness in advance of the impending Roman siege, according to the Lord's command (Matt. 24:16-19). The remnant of her seed (v. 17) are Jewish and Gentile Christians throughout the world, especially among the seven churches of Asia, the targets of attack in 13:7, late in the first century, during a time of tribulation which would greatly intensify over the next two hundred years under the emperors Trajan, Maximus, Decius and Diocletian (Rev. 7:14).

And when he was come nigh, even now at the descent of the Mount of Olives, the whole multitude of the disciples began to rejoice and praise God with a loud voice for all the mighty works that they had seen; saying, Blessed be the King that cometh in the name of the Lord : peace in heaven, and glory in the highest.

And when he was come near, he beheld the city and wept over it, saying, If thou hadst known, even thou, at least in this thy day, the things that belong to thy peace! but now they are hid from thine eyes.—*S. Luke* xix. 37. 38. 41. 42.

MOUNT OF OLIVES FROM THE ROOFTOPS OF JERUSALEM

Chapter Fourteen

THE LATTER DAYS

THE LATTER DAYS" is a famous expression found several times in both Jewish scripture and apostolic writings, as well as in the Dead Sea Scrolls and Jewish non-canonical literature. This phrase has been the source of much religious speculation. Most fundamental evangelical groups refer the mesmerizing phrase "latter days" to a future time period of the earth's existence, immediately before the final return of Christ, popularly called the "second coming," when He allegedly would set up an earthly thousand year reign. One millennial group, the Mormons, embodies that phrase in their official church name – "Latter-day Saints."

Amillennialists and others see the "latter day" biblical passages as being fulfilled by the ministry of Jesus Christ and the gospel era that followed, leading up to the end of the Jewish nation with the destruction of the city of Jerusalem in AD 70. To them the term under discussion is exclusively messianic, allegedly a technical term for the Christian age. Thus, Old Testament passages mentioning the latter days find fulfillment in the generation of Christ and beyond, even to the present day.

Some scholars see various "latter days" passages as coinciding with the final centuries of the existence of the Jewish state, from the time of the release of the Jews after Babylonian captivity in 516 B.C. past the birth and death of Christ until Judea fell to the Romans. All things had to be fulfilled which were written by the prophets about the Jews returning from Babylonian captivity until the coming of Christ, the gospel, the restoration of all things, and the fall of Jerusalem (Luke 24:44; Acts 3:21). Soon after Pentecost, Peter declared to a Jewish audience that "Yea and all the prophets from Samuel and them that followed after as many as have spoken they also told of these days" (Acts 3:24). The suffering of Christ (v. 18) and of the "times of restoration of all things" (v. 21) under one shepherd all transpired during the time of "these days" – Christ's generation (v. 24).

An important consideration is that the Hebrew expression which is often translated "the latter days" is better rendered "in the days to come" or "in the future," as expressed in *The New English Bible, The Jerusalem Bible,* and other translations. Therefore, the phrase can refer to the future generally, or an indefinite long time.

The last (or latter) days, or the end of days, are all common expressions found throughout Jewish intertestamental literature. The author of a *Commentary on Isaiah,* found in the Dead Sea Scrolls, identified the "rod from the stem of Jesse and a Branch shall grow out of its roots. . ." (11:1-3) as the "Branch of David, who shall arrive at the end [of days] . . ," plainly a messianic application. Similar documents, the *Commentary on Nahum,* as well as the famous *I Enoch,* use the term "the last days". The *Testament of Judah* reports that "in the books of Enoch for the righteous [are recorded] the evil things you will do in the last days."

The highly apocalyptic *II Esdras (IV Ezra),* written at the close of the first century, constantly refers to the "end of the age" which he thought was close at hand (2:34). The author also used such phrases as "the age is hastening swiftly to its end" (4:26), the "last times" (6:34), or "end of times" (14:5), as the "completion" (11:44) of the destruction of the Roman Empire (11-13; compare Daniel 7), together with the coming of a redeemer. A companion apocalypse, *II Baruch,* which was written in about AD 90, explains that his teachings were to be kept to "the end of times" (76:2-3; see also 76:5).

Evidently, the widely discussed "latter days" has *no* uniform application, so its meaning must always be determined by context. It is unwarranted to conclude that each occurrence of "latter days" always applies to either the messianic age or to the future end time. It is equally unscriptural to justify a premillennial fulfillment of the "latter day" passages, first to the Jewish end-times in the gospel era of the first century, then to Christ's return at the future end time.

Isaiah 2:2-4 – Micah 4:1-3

Perhaps the most famous scripture that uses the phrase "the latter days" is Isaiah 2:2-5 (Mic. 4:1-3). These prophets declared that in the latter days the "mountain of Yahweh's house [temple – Mic. 3:12-4:1] shall be established on top of the mountains, and shall be exalted above the hills; and all nations shall flow unto it. And many people shall go and say, 'Come ye, and let us go up to the mountain of Yahweh, to the house of the God of Jacob; and He will teach us of His ways, and we will walk in His paths.' For out of Zion shall go forth the law and the word of Yahweh from Jerusalem."

Several views are extant as to what these prophets meant. The proper messianic application treats these words as prophetically declaring that the gospel of Christ would be preached unto all the nations, beginning from Jerusalem or Zion (Luke 24:47). More importantly, the author of Hebrews states that God's people already have come to Mount Zion

(12:22). "Wherefore, receiving a kingdom that cannot be shaken . . ." (12:28) would fulfill the mountain of Jehovah's house which would be established on top of the mountains (Isa. 2:2; see also 27:13b). God's kingdom (rule) is indeed above all earthly governments, and after His resurrection and ascension to the right hand of God, Jesus had already begun His reign from the heavens as prophesied by David (Psa. 2:8-9). This rule continues to this day.

The first Christian writer to apply Isaiah's words to the apostles and their mid-first century evangelistic efforts is Justin Martyr, in about AD 160 (*First Apology,* Ch. 39). Justin stated that Isaiah 2:2-5 was fulfilled by twelve illiterate men of no ability in speaking, yet "by the power of God they proclaimed to every race of men that they were sent by Christ to teach to all the world the word of God . . ." Others later followed Justin's lead, including Irenaeus (see *Against Heresies,* IV:34.4).

The words of Isaiah 2:2-5 probably saw initial fulfillment among covenant people during the era after the Jews returned from Babylonian captivity, "in the future" (the latter days). The prophet preached and wrote around the time of the Assyrian invasion of Judea in about 700 B.C., when armies reached the outskirts of Jerusalem, the "neck" of the city (8:8). The northern kingdom (Israel) had fallen about twenty years earlier, so Isaiah was trying to encourage the covenant faithful in the southern capital to carry out their charge of taking God's moral teaching to the surrounding nations, and if possible bring them to repentance, as in Isaiah 49:3 and 52:13, scriptures later fulfilled more gloriously in the person of Jesus Christ. For Judea, such a noble spiritual intent was a prominent theme in the Psalms, as in 66:1-7, 67:2-5, 86:8-9, 99:2-3, 102:15-16, 105:1f, 117:1.

Thus, Jerusalem would be spiritually exalted before the nations (2:2), an ideal set forth as in Isaiah 60:3, "nations will come to your light," (see also 19:19-20), and many times elsewhere by other prophets (for example, Jer. 3:17, 12:14-17, 16:19; Zeph. 2:11, 3:9; Zech. 8:22, 14:16f). Many of these verses also have messianic import. In Isaiah's blissful vision (2:2-5) he confidently foresaw and end to idolatry and the turning of the heathen to Zion, thus emphasizing the idea of a universal Creator. But these notions were by no means fully realized in Old Testament times, as the peoples' low spiritual condition in the writings of the post-exilic prophets and historical writers amply shows.

Note also that the "mountain of Jehovah's house" (2:2; Micah 4:1) contrasts with the physical destruction of the temple on Mount Moriah, the "mountain of the house" in the previous verse (Micah 3:12b). Contextually, the two phrases have the same meaning; the "mountain" is where the temple building stood. Spiritualizing the "mountain of Jehovah's house" by applying it *exclusively* to the Mount Zion of Hebrews 12:22, the New Jerusalem of the Christian era, is to remove that phrase from its historical context.

Isaiah recognized that the issuance of the law from Zion, the establishment of Jehovah's house on top of the mountains, and the other high hopes of 2:2-5 would be dependent upon the actions of the "house of *Jacob. . .* walking in the light of the Lord" (v.5; comp. with Psa. 14:7, 53:6, 78:68 and Isa. 30:19, 46:15, 64:10). It is not only the future people of Christ walking, but also faithful covenant Jews in the "latter days" – those centuries after their restoration from Babylonian bondage, in 536 B.C.

And so, the "latter days" of Isaiah 2 and Micah 4 is also properly rendered "in the future" or "in [the] days to come," as in *The New English Bible* and *The Jerusalem Bible,* when Yahweh will "judge between the nations" (2:4), fulfilled by Jesus in His own time (see John 5:22-23). Perhaps the most defensible conclusion is admittance of these scriptures having been realized initially during the time God's people returned from Babylonian captivity, then later more gloriously in the messianic age in the first century. A yet future application of Isaiah 2:2-4, with the above fulfillments serving as mere preludes, is speculative at best.

The prophet Isaiah used still another phrase,"latter time," contrasting it with the "former time" in reference to Israel's two most northerly tribes, Zebulun and Nephtali (9:1). These were brought into contempt in Isaiah's day, because they had fallen early to the Assyrians, in about 722 B.C. But, in the "latter time," both would be in messianic glory as the place where Jesus would begin his preaching and teaching (Matt. 4:13). Indeed, that region was the first to see the light (v. 16), and Isaiah in 9:2 had declared that this would happen in the "latter time," in Jesus' day, so it does not await a future fulfillment.

Genesis

Jacob's prophecy concerning his sons (Gen. 49:1f) told what would happen "in the latter days," the earliest biblical occurrence of the phrase. Jacob declared that the scepter would not depart from Judah until Shiloh should come (v. 10). Often thought to foretell the Messiah, the general context (vv. 2-27) shows a fulfillment when the twelve tribes settled Canaan, in the days of Joshua and afterwards. Also, if Shiloh is the person Jesus, how does one account that "his eyes shall be red with wine" (v. 12)? Verses 7-10, 13-21 discuss tribal possessions that applied even to the days of David.

The "latter days" to Jacob, then, meant "the days to come," or in the future. Further, no New Testament writer assigned any statement in Genesis 49 to Jesus or His kingdom. If there is such an application, then it would be that the Jewish nation would not cease existence until after Jesus had come, in the first century, where the "obedience of the people [would] be" (v. 10b).

Numbers

In Numbers 24:14, Balaam told what "this people [Israel] shall do to thy people in the latter days." At that time a "star would rise out of Jacob" (24:17). This person, King David, would break down neighboring nations, especially Moab and Edom. Therefore, the "latter days," for Moses and Balaam, could only be when strife and hindrances would be removed by overcoming enemies, "in times to come" in the era of David. If the star points to Messiah, as many commentators suggest, it would mean that the "latter days" were again fulfilled or perhaps extended an extra 1000 years or so.

Deuteronomy

In Deuteronomy 4, Israel is exhorted to observe God's law. Israel would be long in the land (v. 25), though destruction would come when they would corrupt themselves, and idolators would be scattered (v. 27), driven to serve wood and stone images. But, when judgment would come upon the people in the "latter days," they would return to Yahweh (v. 30) after the exilic experience in Babylon. God would not forget the covenant which He swore unto the fathers (v. 31b). Nevertheless there may be still another application of Deuteronomy 4 in the first century messianic era, when many thousands of Jews brought themselves in subjection to Christ.

Just prior to speaking the farewell song to the assembly of Israel (Deut. 31:30-33:43), Moses predicted that evil would befall the people in the "latter days" (Deut. 31:29). This general prophecy may have come to pass in the tribulation and distress attendant to Jerusalem in the Jewish Wars prior to the fall of Jerusalem in AD 70, although it may be argued just as strongly that latter days means "in days to come," fulfilled in events within the speaker's immediate historical perspective.

Jeremiah

Jeremiah assured the people that "in the latter days ye shall understand it perfectly" (23:20), an apparent fulfillment in the lifetime of Jeremiah, after the fall of Jerusalem in 586 B.C. False prophets contemporary with Jeremiah were speaking lies and vanities, while at the same time Jeremiah was foretelling the doom of Judah and its captivity by Babylon (vv. 16-32).

In 30:24 the understanding promised in the "latter days" would not come at the future "second coming," but would be present in the Jews' return from exile in 536 B.C. Judgment would be brought upon Judah by the Chaldeans. Nevertheless, complete understanding and fulfillment of the prophet's words would come *only* when the Messiah revealed all truth throughout the mid-first century and executed Yahweh's "fierce anger " against Judea in AD 70, as expressed in verse 24.

Jeremiah also mentions the phrase "latter days" two other times and on each occasion they refer to the generation of Christ. He said that prideful Moab "would be brought back in the latter days" (48:47); in the first century many from Moab entered into covenant relationship with the Lord. The same spiritual promise was extended to Elam (49:39). However, these promises also saw limited fulfillment in the time of Cyrus and afterwards, for Moab rallied for five centuries, prospering until the first century before Christ.

Ezekiel

Ezekiel 38 prophesies of unregenerate Gog and its overthrow. Gog is personified as a person, the "Prince of Rosh," and a leader of a great army which would invade the land of Israel in the last time. Of Gog, the prophet promises that "in the latter years thou [Gog] . . . shalt come into the land . . . in the latter days I will bring thee against my land" (vv. 8, 16), so that the nations may know me . . ," a vindication of God's name (38:21, 39:6).

The period of the "latter days" or "years to come" embraces events surrounding the exiled Jews, people "brought back from the nations" (v. 8b). The prophet saw the return of the Jews to their homeland in future years, in fact, in 536 B.C. The words of Ezekiel 38 found further fulfillment in the messianic era, when heathens (Gentiles) "came into the [spiritual] land," becoming God's covenant people through obedience to the Christ and His gospel. See also Revelation 20:7-8, where Gog is a concept which symbolizes the earthly nations banding together to make an assault on God.

Daniel

Daniel revealed to the great Babylonian monarch Nebuchadnezzar what would be in the "latter days" (2:28), the messianic era. Daniel interpreted the king's dream, which tells of a mighty image, bright and terrible (v. 31). Four kingdoms would arise, and, in the days of the crushing, subduing kingdom (the Roman Empire), the God of heaven would set up a kingship in the time of Messiah, in the "latter days" or "days to come."

These events would occur while the Roman Empire was in existence – in fact, in the first century, not in a time yet future. Daniel also said that understanding would befall the people in the "latter days" (10:14) – "in the future" – which began in the third year of the Persian king Cyrus (10:1). It extended to the time of Antiochus Epiphanes (11:21f), an obvious pre-messianic fulfillment. The nature of the understanding is imprecise.

The "time of the end" (Dan. 12:4) and the "end of the days" (v. 13) refers to the close of the period of the four kingdoms discussed earlier by Daniel. It is the first century termination of the Jewish rule and their tribulations. However, the "time of the end" mentioned in 8:17 and the latter time of verse 23 appear to refer to a contemporary period of Hebrew history, in the fourth and third centuries before Christ.

Hosea

Hosea assures us that the children of Israel "would come with fear unto Yahweh . . . in the latter days" (3:5), when a king of the family of David would once again reign over God's people. As faithful Jews responded to apostolic preaching, Israel's messianic hope was realized. Truly, then, Israel and Judah would experience a reunion far more glorious than at the time of their restoration after Babylonian captivity, as promised through the Branch of righteousness, Jesus Christ, the prophetic "David" of Jeremiah 33:15-16, 26 and Ezekiel 34:23-24.

Apostolic References

In Acts 2:17-21, Peter on Pentecost day quoted Joel's famous prophecy which declares that "afterwards" (Joel 2:28) God would pour out his spirit on all flesh, in the last days (2:17). In saying "this is that," Peter saw a fulfillment of Joel. In other words *this* speaking in tongues is a manifestation of the outpouring of the Holy Spirit, *that* which was mentioned by Joel (2:28-32). The apostle thus fixed the latter days to a time period in the first century which embraced the Pentecost of Acts 2.

Joel's "afterward" (or last days), as reiterated by Peter, refers to the same period as the expression, "at the end of these days," used by the author of Hebrews (1:2) which is the period of time when God would be speaking to man through His Son (1:1). Fulfillment took place both in Jesus' ministry and that of the apostles, which followed. The author wrote

Hebrews so that the saints would remain steadfast and not lose confidence, in the turbulent period toward the end of the days of the Jewish kingdom, in the years 66-70. James warned the dispersed twelve tribes about the folly of laying up treasures in the last days (5:3) – the time before the end of the nation.

A few "later-time" references point to events past the year 70, but none of them apply to still-future premillennial events. John's first epistle warns of antichrists in the last hour (2:18-22, 4:3; see also II John 7). These are likely the ubiquitous Gnostic heretics, which appeared toward the end of the first century and plagued orthodox Christians into the second century (and later). Religious writers who thoroughly condemned Gnosticism include Irenaeus, Hippolytus, and Eusebius.

The phrase "in the last time" as used in Jude 18, "in later times" (I Tim. 4:1), and "in the last days" (II Tim. 3:1), all probably refer to the same general period early in the second century. Finally in II Peter 3:3, the author warned of mockers in the "last days" (literally, the "last of these days"), fulfilled either at the time of mockers at a presence (coming) of Christ in second or third century events (probably in connection with Roman persecutions) or which awaits fulfillment at the return of Christ in the undeterminable future.

Summary

The popular religious expression "the latter days" or last of the days, or days to come, finds meaning in various events from the time the children of Israel settled Canaan, during the period of the Babylonian captivity, and afterwards in the first century messianic era. No latter-day reference awaits an exclusive yet-future fulfillment.

Just as the premillennial use of "latter days" erroneously focuses upon one generation of people prior to Christ's "second coming," the concept also does not uniformly apply to the messianic age. More often than not, Old Testament references to the latter days find fulfillment in "days to come" or "in times to come" – events involving the Jewish nation during the four centuries prior to the birth of Christ. In other cases the words "latter days" point to a messianic context.

A scripture employing the term "latter days" may transcend both the late Jewish period and the messianic era. The building of Jehovah's house, which Isaiah saw as occurring "in times to come" among the Jews after their exilic experience, was also fulfilled in the first century gospel expansion, in a messianic climax. Further, the building of God's house and the pouring forth of the law from Zion (Isa. 2:2-4) has an abiding effect which continues to the present time.

Similarly, the many types of blessings mentioned in Joel 2:28-32 (Acts 2:17-21) are not limited only to first century miraculous manifestations (or perhaps even earlier), but extend throughout the centuries, because God's Spirit still administers works of righteousness in His temple (Eph. 2:21-22). Otherwise, the body of Christ on earth is presently dead because of the principle that a body without a spirit is dead (see Jas. 2:26).

The author of Hebrews stated that "at the end of these days" God has spoken through His Son (1:2), a work that is not confined solely to the apostles' proclamation of Christ. The speaking has continued among two millennia of God-fearers, even as God's "living waters," which flowed from sea to sea from Jerusalem before and during the first century (Zech. 14:8-9), did not abruptly dry up in the messianic period (AD 33-70), but rather had a dynamic effect upon righteous people over the centuries to the present. Similarly, the blood of Christ flowed in all directions after the cross, throughout the ages. Evidently, God is interested in the salvation of both Jews and Greeks, before and after the long-fulfilled messianic latter days, and holding the body of Christ together under divine spiritual direction until time is no more.

Chapter Fifteen

CONCLUSION

THE DIVINE VISITATION (Luke 19:44), or presence *(parousia)*, of Jesus Christ, "coming" in judgment against the evil generation of first century Jews, was amply fulfilled in the capture and sacking of Jerusalem in AD 70, by the Roman legions under Titus. It was a brutal and violent catastrophe, one which nearly exterminated the Jewish race (Matt. 24:22). For the Christ, it was a day in which He inflicted vengeance, in the same way Yahweh did in visiting Babylon (Isa. 13), Egypt (Isa. 19), and other ancient heathen nations, such as Edom and Assyria. Divine intervention was felt among the nations, as God delivered the righteous and punished evildoers.

These centuries-old warnings of judgment upon Israel were first uttered by Moses (in Deuteronomy 28), who declared that a swift nation would come upon the people if they rebelled against Yahweh. Verses 52-57, which prophesy a siege against them, were fulfilled explicitly by the Romans, and the "scattering" and the "selling into slavery," all came to pass. The Jews were tossed to and fro among the nations (v.25).

Isaiah told of a day of vengeance, and of judgment against Jerusalem by fire. Joel prophesied that God's spirit would be poured upon all flesh prior to the great and terrible day when He would destroy the city. Before that same day of judgment, Malachi said that Jesus would come in the spirit of Elijah. Daniel foretold the "abomination of desolation," which Jesus said would signal the time when the disciples should flee to safety, before the beginning of the great tribulation that ended with the Roman capture of Jerusalem.

At the start of Jesus' personal ministry, about the year 30-31, John the Baptist warned the Jews of the wrath to come (Matt. 3:7-12). Even then, Jesus was pictured as One holding a winnowing fan which would be used to sift Israel and judge the disobedient. Both John and Jesus proclaimed the grace-filled message that the kingdom of God was at hand.

In His last discourse before the crucifixion, on the Mount of Olives, Jesus revealed how God's retribution would come. Matthew 24 is heavy with warnings of judgment, as are other final or farewell discourses in the Bible. Jacob's prophetic discourse about his sons (Gen. 49), Moses' song to the assembly of Israel (Deut. 32), Paul's exhortation to the elders at Ephesus (Acts 20:29ff), the second letter to Timothy, and II Peter, all fit a common pattern.

In an impressive series of parables and scriptural illustrations, Jesus publicly declared that the kingdom of God would be taken away from the rebellious, Talmudic Jews, who were denounced as "an adulterous and sinful generation" (Matt. 16:4). Privately, Jesus told His disciples that within a generation the city would be taken and the national temple would be dismantled stone by stone (Matt. 24:3). It was like predicting the end of modern Chicago or Dallas.

A series of definite signs would warn the disciples when the crisis in Jerusalem would culminate. The city would be encompassed by armies (Luke 21:20), and the profane Jewish Zealots would stand in the holy place (Matt. 24:15). There would be great political unrest, religious apostasy, civil disturbances, and various natural calamities, including earthquakes, famines, and plagues. Tribulation would come upon Jerusalem. The disciples would be persecuted for upholding the name of Christ. But in their steadfastness He promised spiritual and physical deliverance from the terrible fate of the nation.

The Master's last discourses also denounced the hypocrisy and the wickedness of the institutional Jewish hierarchy, whose writings in the Talmud were based on man-made tradition (see Mark 7:9, 13). Offended by His claims of authority and His foreboding references to the end of their nation, the religious leaders among the Jews arranged for His arrest and crucifixion. The plot quickly thickened against Jesus, and He kept aloof from the rulers until Judas betrayed Him into their hands. An apocryphal temple inscription declared that "Jesus, the king who never reigned, was crucified by the Jews, because He foretold the end of the city and the utter destruction of the temple."

But Jesus rose victoriously from the grave, and 37 years later brought vengeance upon the apostate nation, "that all things which are written may be fulfilled" (Luke 21:22). First, Jerusalem would be surrounded, with the besieged people undergoing terrible and violent suffering. The city would be "trodden down" and multitudes would "fall by the edge of the sword" (Luke 21:24), with their blood mingled with the offerings of heathen sacrifices (Luke 13:1).

Others would be crushed to death from crumbling buildings (Luke 13:4); still thousands more even in their near-starved condition would be led away captive into various Roman provinces. All had been amply warned by Jesus—repent or perish (Luke 13:3, 5)—and those who hearkened to the saving message escaped the great tribulation which came upon Jerusalem. Since they were often exposed to Jesus' saving message during the early gospel era, many turned to Christ. However, by the middle of the decade of 60, some messianic Jews experienced persecution by being cast out of synagogues. Some were even killed after being tortured.

Jesus emphasized how terrible was His judgment against Jerusalem by employment of highly poetic figures: the sun would turn dark like coarse black cloth, the moon would become as red as blood, and the stars would drop to earth as a fig tree letting forth fruit in season (Matt. 24:29). These powerful Oriental images, all with Old Testament counterparts, left a deep impression upon His followers, for obedient Christians during those troubled times saved their lives by contemplating the "signs of the times," and fleeing from the city before the tribulation began.

In those utterances of the ultimate fate of Jewish national life, Jesus furnishes ample evidence of His divine foreknowledge of earthly events. Jesus uttered these prophecies in about AD 32-33, while the province of Judea enjoyed peace with Rome, with no hint of possible war between them. The Romans had a military presence sufficient to keep the people in subjection. Yet, within a generation afterward, Jerusalem revolted against the Romans and the city was violently taken, precisely as Jesus had foretold. Of the glorious temple, "not one stone would be left upon another" (Matt. 24:3), an old saying signifying complete destruction.

As the years passed toward the beginning of the Jewish War in AD 66, the disciples could compare the stirring events taking place to the Master's utterances circulating as oral tradition about famines, the appearance of earthquakes, wars, and the abomination of desolation. As sign after sign appeared, the faithful knew that Jerusalem's days were numbered. The early church historian, Eusebius, wrote that Christ's followers safely departed in haste well before Titus' final siege began in April of AD 70. Josephus noted that many influential people left the city after Gallius' siege four years earlier, in the Spring of the year 66.

During this time of tribulation, the disciples remembered Jesus' warning to flee to the mountains (Matt. 24:16-19), "for when you see Jerusalem encompassed with armies, you know that the time is near" (Luke 21:20), an event fulfilled by the

Romans in the year 66 and also in the spring of AD 68, when the treacherous Idumaean warriors remained encamped around the city walls for several weeks.

Unbelievers and the fainthearted who did not watch for Jesus' signs, were trapped when the city was besieged by Titus less than two years later. Jerusalem fell at the end of that summer. More than the destruction of a city, the temple with its rituals, precious genealogies, and magnificent auxiliary buildings were leveled, never to be rebuilt. Indeed, these were days of divine vengeance, so that all which the Jewish prophets had said concerning these days would be fulfilled (Luke 21:22).

Jesus described it all with the startling accuracy of an eyewitness. Interwoven with the statements about the judgment of Jerusalem was the foretelling of His own betrayal, trial, crucifixion and resurrection, and of the coming of the Holy Spirit, the division His message would cause, and the persecution and death of His followers. By prophesying the end of the Jewish state, Jesus fulfilled His promise of being with His people always, "even to the consummation of the age" (Matt. 28:20). According to His promise, Christ will return personally and visibly in glory to raise the dead and judge all men in righteousness. Contrary to millennial teachings, these end time events will not be preceded by a tribulation period or a thousand-year reign of Christ from a throne in a restored Jerusalem.

Truly, the destruction of Jerusalem is a consistent, valuable biblical theme. Many scriptures referring to the end of the Jewish time are not immediately apparent because of confusion of the various "comings" of the Lord Jesus Christ. In earlier times, a Jewish prophet's announcement of a "coming" always referred to a destruction of a temporal heathen nation, or a chastisement of Israel or Judah. In many specific instances as King of the nations, Yahweh came and descended upon ancient societies which were ripe for judgment. Such events were described in apocalyptic figures, through the use of celestial objects and radical language.

Now, as King of kings and heir to all things (Heb. 1:1) and as One possessing all authority (Matt. 28:18), Jesus still presides over the nations and according to His will, determines their rising and their falling. Any ancient or modern intervention is a *parousia,* the power of Christ and His influence in earthly events. Throughout Matthew 24, Jesus employed longstanding oriental figures and imagery to foretell His coming against Jerusalem within a generation (v. 34), as a manifestation of His rule. That godly judgment was rendered upon disobedient, gainsaying Jerusalem in AD 70, is confirmed by several Jewish prophets, and all first century gospel writers. Divine vengeance did not delay in visiting the Jewish nation, to inflict punishment upon them for their iniquity in crucifying the Christ of God, and acting as a stumbling block among His followers.

Subject Index

Abomination of Desolation, 47, 50, 51, 71 78; explained, 90-4, 99, 180, 182
"All the world", 75, 170
"All these things", 86
Amorites, 70
Angels (messengers), 57, 68, 77
Antichrist, 47, 160, 177
Antiochus Epiphanes, 30, 175
Antonia, Tower of, 21, 122, 123
Apocalyptic literature, 41, 164
Apostasy (as sign of end-time), 15, 18, 88, 89, 167-7, 160, 161, 180
Assyria, 23, 30, 127, 179

Babylon, 23, 24, 30, 32, 34, 37, 66, 84, 100, 130, 134, 135, 136, 141, 143, 160, 173, 174, 179
Barcochebus, 126
Belshazzar, 160
Birth pangs (symbol of new order), 17, 86

Calamity (catastrophe), 14, 32, 86, 101, 128, 133, 138, 154, 157, 158, 179
Cannibalism, 30
Cestius Gallius, 20, 113, 115, 125
Church fathers cited, 87, 89, 93, 94, 96, 158, 159, 170
Claudius (Roman emperor), 84
Clouds (symbol of judgment), 13, 14, 16, 18, 23, 25, 65, 80, 85, 133-4, 139-42, 155, 156
Coming, 23, 28, 48, 78, 81-2, 132-3, 162-4, 179, 186; see also Presence
Consolation of Israel, 16
Consummation of the age, 76-7, 89, 134, 183
Correspondence (principle of), 37, 137
Covenant (gracious agreement with God), 30, 46, 52, 55, 60, 61, 69, 91, 130, 142, 151, 162; Covenant curses, 29, 71
Cyrus (Persian king), 48, 50, 130, 174, 175

Darkness (symbol of judgment), 37-8, 135, 137; see also Clouds, Moon, Stars, Sun.
Day of darkness (sunless day, symbol of judgment), 135-7
Day of decision, 38
Day of the Lord (Day of Yahweh, symbol of judgment), 18, 37, 38, 137
Dead Sea, 113, 119
Deliverance, 41, 45, 60, 100, 108, 126, 127, 140, 142, 181; see also Escape
Desolate, 20, 30, 48, 49, 50, 51, 71, 90, 130
Disease, 29, 96

Eagle (symbol of Israel's enemy), 30, 129-32
Earthquakes (sign of end-time), 14, 24, 34, 57, 75, 84, 85, 96, 99, 144, 181, 182
Edom, 38, 134, 173, 179
Egypt, 23, 24, 31, 34, 83, 84, 104, 119, 132, 136, 139, 151, 152, 179
Eleazer, 110
"Elijah" (John the Baptist), 40
"Elijah" (Jesus), 39, 51, 180
End of the world, 75, 76, 77, 89, 135
End-time (time of the end), 22, 25, 26, 41, 46, 47, 51, 52, 96, 100, 104, 134, 136, 137, 139, 148, 158, 161, 169, 183
Epidemics, 22,
Escape (deliverance, flight to safety), 22, 37-9, 51, 94, 105, 118, 120, 154, 165
Ethiopia, 23, 139
Eusebius, (church historian) quoted, 82, 84, 126, 138, 177, 182

False teachers (appearances at end-time), 14, 75, 88, 147
Famine, 21, 75, 84, 94, 105-7, 110, 124
Fan, winnowing fan, fork (symbol of judgment), 54, 64, 180

Fig tree (symbol of Israel), 65, 66, 102,
144, 150, 182
Figurative language, *see* Hyperbole;
Symbols and Symbolic Language
Fire (symbol of destruction), 24, 34, 35,
37, 39, 53, 58, 157, 158
Flames (symbol of destruction), 21, 24, 34,
35, 77, 87, 108, 126, 127, 161
Four winds, 85, 143, 144
Full end (of Jews), 31, 48, 49, 50, 135

Gather, 70, 142-143
Genea (generation), 149, 150
Generation (of Jerusalem's destruction), 15,
20, 27, 54, 57, 67-70, 147-154
Gessius Florus, 113
Gods (office holders), 21, 160-1
Gog, 174-5
Gospel to all the world (sign of end-time),
75, 89
Great Tribulation, 181; described, 99-124

Hailstones, 24
Heaven and earth, 34-6, 152-3
Heavens (symbol of political nations) 24,
133-45
Heavens, darkened or trembling (symbol of
political upheaval), 133-6
Herod (Judean king), 73, 87, 108, 122
Hills, 85, 120, 134, 156, 157, 169; *see also*
Mountains
Hyperbole (language of judgment), 100-1

Idumaeans, 92, 116-7, 125
"Immediately", 15, 18, 45, 133, 148, 167
Israel (modern state), 31, 104, 150-2

Jerusalem (siege of), described, 20-1, 73-4,
105-10, 120-4
map, 121
Jesus, as Judge, 12, 27, 59-60; as King, 11-
3, 18, 19, 42-4, 60, 65; foreknowledge
of, 182-3; final return of, 25-7, 153,
158-9, 167, 169
Jewish citations (non-canonical), 79, 85,
91, 101, 132, 136, 138, 139, 144, 154,
168-9
Jewish Wars, (AD 66-74), 15, 18, 20, 97,
101, 103-24, 173
John the Baptist, 33, 35, 39, 40, 53, 56, 62,
64, 67, 69, 127, 143, 180

Josephus, Flavius (Jewish historian), 21, 31,
73, 74, 81, 82, 83-5, 93, 101, 114,
115-7, 119, 125, 127, 182; describes
Great Tribulation, 104-10
Judicial coming, 15

Kingdom of God (reign of heaven, divine
power, rule of Christ over hearts) , 16-7,
41-7, 54-7, 61, 63, 80, 114, 144, 149,
180; *see also* Reign

"Latter days", 18, 31, 82, 150, 167-78
"Let the reader understand", 94
Lightning, 14, 127, 128, 133, 141
"Little horn" (of Daniel), 136

Man of sin, 159, 160, 161
Masada, 110, 113, 124
Medo-Persians, 23
Milleniallism, 12, 14, 18, 26, 41-2, 47, 75,
81, 90, 96-7, 100, 137, 145, 150-1, 177
Moab, 31, 173, 174
Moon (lightless, symbol of temporal
judgment), 37, 133-8, 145, 164, 182
Mount of Olives, 32, 33, 74, 82, 180
Mountains (symbol of political
government), 33, 85, 94, 95, 97, 99,
104, 114, 129, 134, 135-6, 156, 157,
169, 170, 171, 182
Mountains falling, trembling (symbol of
political upheaval), 85, 134, 135, 136
Mourning of Jewish tribes, 34, 141
Mt. Olivet, *see* Mount of Olives

Nations (shaking of, symbol of judgment),
134-7, 162-3; *see also* Heavens, Shaking
Nebuchadnezzar (Nebuchadrezzar), 30, 33,
66, 160, 175
Nero (Roman emperor), 87, 89
Ninevah, 68

Parallelism, 11, 76, 157
Parousia, 15, 17, 23, 76-80, 142, 147, 154,
158, 159, 164, 179, 184;
see also Coming, Presence
Partial fulfillment of prophecy, 47, 90
Pella (Roman city), 89, 105, 117
Pentecost (of Acts 2), 12, 17, 36, 37, 42,
45, 51, 52, 56, 80, 137, 168, 176
Pestilence, 84, 94, 96, 110; *see also* Disease,
Epidemics

SCRIPTURE INDEX

BOOKS BY NEVADA PUBLICATIONS
Write to address below for prices and a complete catalog.

THAT YOU MAY BELIEVE by Homer Hailey. Subtitled "Studies in the Gospel of John," this book is designed to lay a firm foundation of faith for a consistent Christian life. John's gospel was written to help dispel doubt about the deity of Christ. This topical study is packed with helpful material adequate for individual or group study. 200 pages.

FROM CREATION TO THE DAY OF ETERNITY God's Great Plan to the Day of Eternity by Homer Hailey. This book builds faith in God's system of redemption. God is seen in nature, in providence and in His Christ. Next is a simple retelling of the story of creation, the introduction of man, the home and the fall. Lofty Old Testament themes are evident in the historical section which shows God's hope-inspiring promise, the purpose of law, and Israel's apostasy, captivity and restoration. Later chapters relate Christ's birth, ministry, death, and His resurrection, and also studies on godly character, the church, the "second coming," the resurrection and judgment. A well-written book, easily understood by readers of all ages. Indexed, 226 pages.

HAILEY'S COMMENTS by Homer Hailey, This study touches upon the Exodus, Genesis, the Passover, and the giving of the law. Following a significant article on "Studying the Prophets" are extensive commentaries on Amos, Hosea, Isaiah, Daniel, Ezekiel, and Jeremiah. Next comes Jesus and the virgin birth, His baptism, temptation, transfiguration, the last supper and His prayers. "Comments on Evangelism" furnishes information for both the church and individuals. The author details the nature of the rule of elders. Other chapters involve stewardship, the need for a savior, and the saints amid a secular world, the soul, heaven and hell, suffering, II Peter 3, etc. Vol. I, 347 pages, Vol. II, 384 pages, a matching set with scripture and general indices, color covers.

Upcoming Titles

Manuscripts are completed. Call 702-747-0800 for information.
Advance print-outs of the texts now available for $6 each, postpaid.

◆ Natural Law: Universal in Scope, Moral in Design
◆ The Kingdom of God: A Relationship Not an Institution
◆ The Identity of Babylon as Rome and the Dating of the Book of Revelation – with supplemental material on the "AD 70 Doctrine"
◆ The Nature of Inspiration and the Development of the New Testament Canon ($7.50)
◆ Coping with Church Sharks (A Twelve-Step Guide for Recovery)

NEVADA PUBLICATIONS Box 15444 ◆ Las Vegas, Nev. 89114

THE ETERNAL COVENANT OF PEACE

by Stanley W. Paher

288 pages, color cover

Stanley W. Paher

And a great sign appeared in heaven, a woman clothed with the sun, and on her head was crown of twelve stars . . . Embodied in these words of John the Revelator is the lofty concept of a personage who represents all the Jewish faithful of old and believers in Christ throughout the ages – all enjoying the same gracious saving relationship with God in the eternal covenant. This continuity is reflected in such concepts as kingdom, body and church, as well as in Paul's illustration of the olive tree of Romans 11.

This book begins by defining the nature of covenant and follows with what it militates against: Rabbinic Judaism, which turned God's gracious, saving commitment with man into legalistic, party-centered religion. As God in lovingkindness extended to Abraham the covenant, He promised man a covering for sin and a constant concern for their welfare, spiritual blessings for all nations, Abraham's seed, forever. Through revelations to Moses, the covenant was extended to one people, the children of Israel.

By the time of David the eternal covenant had been renewed and extended with the promise of the coming of the Anointed One. Prophets such as Jeremiah and Ezekiel enlarged covenantal concepts by promising the law in the heart and new hearts and spirits as God interdwelled with man, extending to them the remission of sin. Though Jeremiah and the New Testament author of Hebrews described each of the covenantal terms as "new," they all indeed restated long-established concepts.

In the first century the presence of Christ as the reality and substance of the covenant and His one-time pleasing sacrifice mean that God's agreement with man has reached its final development by embracing the Gentiles. Here is a well written, fresh approach toward a vital subject which the author considers "the marrow of all faith." As Paher aptly states, "Covenanters now enjoy the certainty of salvation because of this positive covenantal relationship. They have drunk of the water given by Christ, and it springs up into everlasting life."